ME — AND THE STAGS

NAOMI JACOB

ME — AND
THE STAGS

WILLIAM KIMBER
46 WILTON PLACE, LONDON S.W.1

First published in 1964 by
WILLIAM KIMBER AND CO. LIMITED
46 Wilton Place, London S.W.1

MADE AND PRINTED IN GREAT BRITAIN BY PURNELL AND SONS, LTD.
PAULTON (SOMERSET) AND LONDON

For
ANGELA DU MAURIER and BETTY SEYMOUR HICKS
to remind them of the days of St. Chad's, with my love.
MICKIE.

CONTENTS

7

"These men are all upper crust here."

(Haliburton)

I

INTRODUCTION

Last year I wrote a book called *Me—and the Swans*; it dealt with various women I have known who have demanded my admiration, my respect and my deep affection. Some of them bore names which are household words, some of the names served to wake memories in the minds and hearts of my readers, some were unknown yet held an important place in my life. In short all of them were "Swans". I have often been told that my geese are all swans, and I have always denied it, insisting that my swans were incomparable, that many of them were exceedingly beautiful, and others made up in brains and warm hearts for what they might lack in actual physical charm.

Before I began that book I knew that I was going to "stand up to be shot at", and I was right! True, there were "bouquets", but there was also a fairly heavy bombardment. Some of the critics were so angry with me for having liked anyone at all that they used the heaviest artillery to attempt to slaughter what was a not very large, not particularly profound book. I felt they must be the kind of people who would take sledge hammers to kill butterflies.

It was borne upon me that if you venture to say that a woman was beautiful, you lay yourself open to a charge of being merely flattering; if you praise any character for their kindliness, their charm, their warm-heartedness, you are accused of being mawkishly sentimental; if you refer to any small failings, irritability, quick temper, intolerance of this or that, then you are told that you are spiteful and making carping criticisms.

As a matter of fact, I have always tried—and this can be applied to people of either sex if you change the pronouns—to

> Be to her virtues very kind,
> Be to her faults a little blind.

Actually, if faults exist, I rarely see them, privately I don't even admit of their existence.

So I read my press cuttings with, I admit, no particular feeling of humiliation, because when all's said and done, the people who decide if a book is worth reading are the members of the public. As, "The drama's laws, the drama's patrons give," so with books. One critic of *Me—and the Swans* assured his readers that it was obvious that the book had given me more pleasure to write, than it would give them to read. Another insisted that the book would have been more worthy of note had I dealt less with the achievements of the characters and more with the development of their mentalities.

A third—I felt that he must have an active personal dislike for me though so far as I know I have never met him—really grew very annoyed indeed. He castigated me for my inferior punctuation. Well, I accepted that, it is not emphatically my strong suit, then he apparently gave up hope for the book, I could imagine him saying, "Why should I waste my time with this woman's rubbish?" He ended his criticism by stating that the book was a piece of "mawkish sentimentality". I admit that parts of it were filled with sentiment, but that any of it was mawkish—well, to be candid, I'm not quite sure what the word means, except that it is something unpleasant.

Despite this, when I suggested to my publisher that I should write about some of the men I have known and admired, he gave his assent immediately. I wanted to call it, *Me—and the* — and there I stuck because I didn't know what the male swan was called. I asked various people, none of them had any ideas on the subject, they just said vaguely, "Well, swans, I suppose." I wrote to Margery Weiner who specializes in discovering the most unlikely things. For example, what Queen Elizabeth the First liked for breakfast, or the name of George Bernard Shaw's favourite dog. Not that I have ever asked for the answer to either of these queries, I have no particular interest in the favourite menus of Elizabeth Tudor, and I rather doubt the existence of Bernard Shaw's dog, favourite or otherwise.

Back came Margery's reply. "Why don't you ask me something really difficult? The male swan is a cob, the female a pen."

Now a cob to me has meant one of two things, a rather large, very excellent nut grown in Kent, or a type of rather stocky, stolid and solid horse, used by elderly gentlemen who prefer safety to speed where horseflesh is concerned. I abandoned the idea of *Me—and my Cobs*, and sought for some other animal. Tigers implied fierce dangerous creatures, lions, "the King of beasts", with a weakness for roaring. They didn't quite satisfy me either. Snakes, monkeys, dogs, cats all seemed worse than useless; then I thought of stags.

Not that my knowledge of stags was in any way profound, I knew that they were "Monarchs of the Glen" because in my days of theatrical touring I had seen the picture bearing that name in many "digs". The stag, with eighteen points no doubt, stood in an attitude of arrogant defiance, its expression was haughty and slightly offensive. You felt that any intruder would be accorded a welcome which would be far from cordial. I knew that stags drank their fill "at eve", for I had seen another picture showing them in the act of doing so. Apparently they drank rather more than their fill, for the water was cascading from their mouths. Still I had among my friends any number who were convivial souls who frequently drank their fill. Others who were slightly haughty, and others who were not over partial to intruders. I decided upon *Me—and the Stags*.

If in this book I have dealt with men who were either members of the theatrical or the music hall professions, if in fact they predominate, remember that a great deal of my exceedingly long life has been spent in theatres and music halls, and my time spent with people who work in them. That is not an excuse, but a reason. I have found members of both these professions interesting as personalities, many of them exceedingly witty, and certainly ninety per cent of them kindly, warm-hearted, and friendly.

Everyone knows that the actor's art is the most transient of all the arts; books, pictures, poems, statues, splendid buildings, wonderful roads all serve as lasting memorials of the men who made them. The actor's masterpieces die with him, except in so far as they live in the memory of his audiences. So the voices of great singers die, for despite the modern excellence of recordings, nothing can actually reproduce the voice, either in the words or singing. Even in records which have done as well as science and invention have made possible, the visual is lacking. So my memories of Henry Ainley, of Sarah Bernhardt, of Ellen Terry, of Caruso, of Gigli, of Tetrazzini are far more capable of bringing back to me vivid memories of the occasions when I heard and saw these great artists, than any record however excellent, produced by mechanical means.

Because I had the privilege of knowing the men of whom I have written, of seeing them on the stage, of talking with them, and seeing them when they were not "servants of the public", I hope that I may have revived memories of them for people who saw them and perhaps knew them as I did.

For those chapters which deal with men who were not of the theatre, I have chosen them because some of them are well known, they have a "public" of their own, they have in some way or another affected the lives, in greater or smaller degree, of hundreds of people. I am thinking here of Bryan Michie, Cecil Roberts and James Norbury.

Two men I have chosen as typical of the best of their different professions. I am not insisting that either of them were brilliant intellectually, though Harding Cartwright was regarded as a very notable and gifted seaman. Don Martino would have smiled had anyone suggested that he was even moderately clever, but he "had something" which made him an outstanding character, and a very great parish priest.

There were other names which I should have liked to include, one was Ivor Novello. His life has been written by that fine chronicler of the stage and member of the theatrical profession, the late Macqueen-Pope. "Popie" said to me that his life of Ivor had been most difficult to write, "it was so hard not to make it just a long list of successes, to write only another success story."

I should have found it equally difficult to write even a short sketch of Ivor Novello; I should have brought down the wrath of those people who dislike to read of anyone being praised or eulogized. Those people who long for a few "buts" and "ifs"—I could not have avoided writing nothing but pleasant, kind, lovable things about Ivor; in so far as his character was concerned less pleasant attributes did not exist.

A man who was in the theatrical profession, once said to me, "It is almost impossible to believe that any man can be so genuinely nice as you know that Jack Warner really and truly is!"

So many of us who knew him felt exactly the same about Ivor Novello. When his will was read, Tom Arnold said, "Ivor has remembered everybody!" and that rather summed up his character.

To return for a moment to Harding Cartwright, Master Mariner. He represented the finest type of Mercantile Marine Officer. Incredibly modest regarding his own achievements, completely generous when recounting those of others. No flag-wagger, no jingo, but a man with that inborn love of his native land and filled with determination to serve her to the utmost of his capacity.

One more thing, and I will leave you to read about my friends. I have not "revealed" anything, I have not "disclosed for the first time" that this one was a confirmed alcoholic, or that one a habitual drug addict. I have not admitted, with a kind of verbal self-satisfied smirk, that one was a complete and utter liar, or another possessed a whole collection of petty meannesses, and was not too scrupulous at cards.

Why not? First of all, it would not be true, for none of the men of whom I have written were any of these things. Secondly, had such things been true, why should I bore myself —and I hope my readers—by writing about them? If I found a man that I considered to be a fine fellow, a great actor, a good friend, why should I dig and delve like a pig rooting for truffles, to find something which would prove that he was in reality something of a blackguard? I don't like unpleasant people, I don't like mean, cruel, base people and I don't want to write about them. As Marie Lloyd used to sing,

> If you like a thing, you like it,
> That's enough!

And that applies to people as well as things!

I have not either the wish or the power to impose my views of these men of whom I have written on anyone. I have written of them as I have known, or as I still know them. To me they were "faithful and just", and I am grateful to them for the delight their work gave me, and for the generous friendship which they accorded—and fortunately for me some of them still accord—to me.

II

DON MARTINO

OST of us in the course of our lives have met various priests, some of us have met priests of all denominations, and we have to admit that they provide a—mixed bag. They have been broad-minded and tolerant, narrow and restricted in their outlook, cheerful and jovial, subdued and humourless, ignorant and bigoted, intellectual and highly erudite.

Many—of various denominations—I have disliked intensely. I may have no fault to find with them when they are the other side of the altar rails, they may deliver excellent sermons in pleasant, educated voices—but "off duty", although I may have respected their uniform, I have detested them as men.

I was brought up almost in the precincts of Ripon Cathedral where my mother had been married and where I was christened. It is recorded that on that occasion I behaved exceedingly badly. My mother was something of an authority on Church Music and believed that even small children should be brought up to attend church regularly, and learn to listen to sermons.

I heard many of the noted preachers of the day—Bishop Boyd Carpenter, Canon MacColl, Bishop Weldon, Dr Lang, then Bishop of Stepney I think and later Archbishop of York. Later I was to hear Father Martingale, Mgr. Robert Hugh Benson, Cardinal Griffin, Cardinal Godfrey, and His Holiness Pope Pius. Some of them I enjoyed listening to, others I considered lamentable; dull, ponderous, and completely given up to the enjoyment of their own voices which, particularly in the case of the Protestant clergy, were invariably very pleasant to the ear.

When I came to live in Italy, in a small village called Sir-mione, more than thirty years ago, I met the Parish Priest, *Reverendo*, as they called him in the village. I remember making my first confession—my first in Italy—to him, in the most halting, incorrect Italian imaginable. Never for a second did he give any sign that what I said was unintelligible, which I am certain that it was! I barely understood one word in twenty when he spoke to me before giving Absolution, but the tone of his voice was essentially kindly, and full of friendly warmth.

I saw him daily walking in the village, tall, handsome, white haired and innately dignified in his shabby cassock, beneath which his large, serviceable boots showed. He always raised his *berretta* and said in a deep full voice, "*Rispetti*——" If I passed him in the early evening walking along the quiet lane which led to the Lake, as I took my beloved Peke for his walk, he would sometimes stop and speak to him, praising his good looks.

At Mass, Don Martino was the essence of dignity, he wore his vestments magnificently, he moved with careful, measured paces, and you could hear every word clearly and distinctly. The church, which is very old, is large and his sonorous, well-modulated voice could be heard clearly wherever you might be sitting.

The liturgy of the Roman Catholic Church is, like that of the English church, both beautiful and dignified, and it is regrettable that so many priests—I am speaking now of Catholic priests—either gabble it as if the lives of the whole congregation depended on ending the Mass as quickly as possible, or else seem to regard the whole of the Liturgy as something which must be kept a profound secret and speak in a voice scarcely above a whisper.

With Don Martino the noble Latin phrases reached you clearly, spoken unhurriedly and distinctly. His preaching, I have to admit, was lamentable. He allowed himself to lapse into broad dialect, he said nothing that was particularly uplifting or comforting. Strictly speaking they were not sermons, for he was not a licensed preacher, they were merely parochial addresses. Even as such one had to admit that they were— pretty poor.

I gathered, as I came to understand Italian, that he was in no way "a power" in the village, true he appealed from time to time for better collections, I remember him once assuring his congregation that the amount of the collection averaged less than a half-penny a head! That he ever extorted money, demanded heavy fees for marriages, funerals and the like, levied fines for misdoings and subsequent absolutions I never heard. I know that in those days the village was poor and many of the people found life something of a struggle. Now Sirmione is a popular holiday resort and practically everyone is sufficiently well off, many people have grown exceedingly rich.

I did learn that if some poor peasant lost one of his two oxen through illness, the first person he called upon for help was his parish priest. Don Martino was a good judge of cattle, would go with the man to give judgement on the value of the ox which he proposed to purchase, and out of his own savings —which must have been pretty meagre—help on the financial side of the purchase.

I know that his stipend was very small indeed, part of it was a small grove of olive trees, and a field adjacent to Sirmione where he grew vines. The olives were carefully gathered, and Don Martino had his own press. I can testify that his olive oil was the best I have ever tasted—clear, rich and smooth. His grapes were harvested, and pressed in the street just opposite to the church, in the old-fashioned way, by treading.

I remember walking up the steep street to my house—which was just opposite to the church—and seeing a lorry on which stood two huge wooden tubs piled high with grapes. I stopped to watch. I saw Luigi Costa, my gardener, a man not exactly noted for his cleanliness, roll up his trousers and leap into one tub and begin—treading. I made a mental note never to drink wine again, but later argued with myself that possibly the wine I was drinking was not the result of Luigi's energetic foot-work—but at the time the sight of wine making—in the raw—shocked me.

The fact remains that the Priest's wine like his olive oil was exceptionally good.

I found out that he came from Malcesine, a village on the Lake-side, his family were respectable small tradesmen and farmers. Don Martino had gone to the Ecclesiastical College in Rome, and when ordained had for a very short time been one of the junior curates at Malcesine. He had then been appointed to the very small parish of Sirmione. He remained there for nearly sixty years.

He lived in the house allotted to the parish priest, opposite to the church. He had an old housekeeper to look after him, and I must say that she kept the place spotlessly clean. His rooms were reached by a wide stone staircase. I have been in his sitting room, which was also where he received visitors, and kept the various registers, many times. I gather that this room and a bedroom were all that he used.

The floor was uncarpeted, with two strips of carpet on either side of a large, solid table. The chairs were of the kind known as kitchen chairs, there were a couple of cheap book cases, and a small, uncomfortable sofa, of that type particularly favoured by poor Italians. It would accommodate two people sitting, but no one could lie down on it. The walls were white-washed, there was a Crucifix hanging on one, and I remember two lithographs of defunct Popes. That was all.

He possessed a ramshackle old bicycle, which he did not ride very well, which he used to reach anyone who was sick and lived outside the actual village.

What struck me most forcibly about Don Martino was the change that seemed to come over the man when he was "vested". You saw him in the street, giving his courteous greeting when he passed anyone he knew, and as he knew everyone he might, at greater convenience to himself, have

carried his *berretta* in his hand! A tall, stout, shabby figure,
with a handsome face and silver hair, sometimes not too
carefully shaved.

I remember once asking him to dinner to meet two friends
of mine who both spoke Italian fluently. I asked which night
would suit him. He considered gravely, then said, "Not Sunday, it is a busy day for me, shall we say Wednesday, signora?
You see I always shave on Saturdays and Wednesdays."

When you saw him, wearing his vestments, his hands holding those elements with which he would administer the Last
Rites of the Church to some dying parishioner, when he walked
in one of the religious processions—for example on Corpus
Domini or Good Friday (*Venerdi Santo*) he seemed to have
taken on a new personality. The elderly, friendly, and rather
matter-of-fact parish priest had vanished, and in his place
you saw a dignified, aloof representative of all that Holy
Church stood for. He was, you felt, conscious of his office,
and proud of it, proud with that humility which recognized
that an honour had been conferred by reason of the recipient's
office and that he recognized that honour with pride.

I never felt that Don Martino officiating at Mass was the
same man who would stroll into my garden, smoking one of
those rather evil smelling Toscani cheroots, accept a cup of
coffee or a glass of wine and talk pleasantly of mundane things,
possibly making one or two rather poor and utterly innocuous
jokes.

Even when he came each Easter to bless my house, once he
began the prayers for the well-being of all the inhabitants of
the villa, he seemed to change. As he walked up the garden
with me, he might smile and snap his fingers in greeting to
Sammy, the Peke, but once he opened his missal—though he
must have known the prayers by heart—he became "a priest
forever after the order of Melchisedech". Once the prayers
were over he would say with a twinkle, "I must bless the kitchen so that the pans will not burn."

His sacristan then handed you four very thin votive candles, and you made your Easter offering. Don Martino shook hands rather ceremoniously and as you walked to the gate with him—he became your good parish priest again.

If I seem to have conveyed that he assumed this change as a kind of "act", I have done my work badly. It was something, I firmly believe, that literally descended on him and enveloped him when he was actively engaged on God's work.

The last time my house was blessed—and I think that the priest was only in the place about seven minutes from his entrance to his exit—my cook said to me, a trifle caustically, "Signora, I hope that Almighty God heard what was said—for I didn't!"

I used to like to watch him at christenings, and as I am god-mother to a number of boys and girls—many of them now grown up and married—I had plenty of opportunity to observe his treatment of them at the font. He held them as babies should be held, quite firmly and steadily, and they rarely cried when in his arms. I once told him that he was over-generous with the Holy Water, that one day he'd kill a baby with the shock. He smiled, "If such a thing happened, the baby would die in a state of perfect Grace and go straight to Heaven as we all know the Holy Innocents did. But——" he added, "if I am generous with the water, I am very sparing with the salt! The *poverini* don't like the taste of it!"

My housekeeper Elsa, who was with me for twelve years and is now married and lives in England, was devoted—as everyone was who came in contact with him—to Sammy. She used to take him to the cinema, and I shall never forget how he dis-liked the film made from that possibly fine, but undeniably dreary, book *Resurrection*. He voiced his disapproval so loudly that Elsa had to bring him out. She said to me, "Not that I blamed him, signora, it was a film full of misery!"

She used to take him to Benediction on Sunday evenings; I asked Don Martino if he objected.

"What right have I to object?" he asked, "if he behaves well and does not disturb other people. I am no Saint Antonio,

22

but he preached to the fishes, and an English Saint *Veelfreed* preached to the seals!" So Sammy continued to go to Benediction, and I always gave him money for the collection.

Now Don Martino had heard me say that Sammy was a Pekinese and doubtless gathered that this meant an inhabitant of Pekin. I have grave doubts if he had any very clear idea as to where Pekin was, but it sounded a far-off, outlandish kind of place anyway!

On one Missionary Sunday, when he was appealing for contributions to foreign missions—though probably the poor man needed the money far more than the heathen did—he addressed the congregation at Benediction, among them Sammy, on the necessity for giving generously.

"There are people in the world," he said, speaking with that particularly bad delivery of his, "who have no knowledge of Our Lord Jesus Christ. For example such people as the *Africani*, the *Indiani*, the *Australiani*, the *Cinesi* and the *Pekinesi*——"

On the following Monday, I met Don Martino, and said, "Padré, you have mortally offended one of your parishioners by something you said in your sermon at Benediction." I told him, adding, "Sammy says that he will never come to Benediction and never contribute another *soldo* to any collection!"

He insisted on coming back to my villa with me, and apologizing very handsomely to Sammy and assuring him that such a thing should never happen again.

Sammy being the gentleman he was, accepted the apology gracefully, saying, "Think no more about it, Padré, my annoyance is a thing which belongs to the past. Let us live in the present and for the future. I shall be in my usual place at your excellent church next Sunday."

The Padré loved entertaining, and being entertained. On one occasion there was some festival in connection with the Church—what it was exactly I have forgotten—and a number of priests were to attend from surrounding parishes, among them a Canon, who was also the Priest in Charge at Desenzano and a person of some considerable importance.

I suppose that there were about ten of them altogether. Don Martino confided to me that his china, glasses and cutlery would not run to it. Half shyly he intimated that possibly I might entertain them. I said that I should be delighted.

He suggested with some hesitation that "Cock-tails Inglese" would be a delightful surprise to follow the tea—which was to be coffee not tea, as preferred by their reverences, who know little of tea, and what they did know—they didn't care for.

I knew that the Padré had already tasted cocktails at my villa, and I suspected that he had boasted of them to his clerical friends, in all probability conveying that they were the national drink of the *Inglese*.

In England we should have called the meal which was offered to their reverences a—nursery tea. Thin bread and butter—not rolls—several kinds of sandwiches, jam tarts, two kinds of cake, and *petit fours* obtained from that excellent shop, Camera's in Brescia.

How they ate, those reverend gentlemen! Don Martino beamed as he saw various huge slices of cake disappear into the mouth of the Canon. That priest confided to me that he spoke "a little English", and proceeded to recite his entire vocabulary.

"MackDon-al'—Baltveen—Keeng Chorch—Prin-sov-Galles—'Ow doo yew do pleze?—feenesh."

I complimented him on his accent.

The table was cleared, the priests drew back their chairs, Don Martino's eyes telegraphed quite plainly, "Cocktails".

The shaker with the glasses on which were painted cocks of brilliant plumage were brought. The glasses in themselves provided a new source of conversation, and the exclamations which followed my statement that a *gallo* was called a cock in English were loud and surprised.

Were these drinks the favourite beverage of cocks? Were they drunk with *gallo arrosto* (Roast fowl)? Did the hens also enjoy them and so on. The cocktails were ordinary dry Martinis, but they were much appreciated, and the Canon gave it as his opinion that this was the right and proper use to which Martini should be put.

It was time for the visitors to go, the empty glasses stood on the low table, there was much handshaking and expressions of thanks. Don Martino, flushed with pleasure at the success of the party, picked up his cloak and prepared to fling it round his shoulders. Few men wore a cloak better than our parish priest. The cloak swung in a wide arc, caught the glasses and eight of them crashing to the tiled floor shattered to bits.

Poor Don Martino, all his happiness was shattered like the glasses, he was overcome with shame, his apologies almost pathetic in their profusion. I protested that it was nothing, and the Canon said almost pontifically, "As this cocktail is much used in England, most certainly there are others in the cupboard!" I assured him that there were—dozens!

So the party ended, and the next morning Don Martino sent me a sack of sweet chestnuts, a smaller one of new walnuts, and several bottles of his own oil and wine. The glasses were never referred to again.

He liked me to take my English friends to visit him, and one evening he invited seven or eight of us to go and take wine with him. He received us in his bare, uncomfortable sitting room, there were several bottles of wine, a collection of wine glasses—not all the same shape or pattern, and a large plate of biscuits. Now Italian biscuits are quite horrible unless you buy the most expensive kinds. Admittedly they have improved of later years, but twenty-five years ago they were soft, stale, either completely tasteless or violently impregnated with vanilla. Added to that they were crumbly and horribly soft. Still, biscuits meant—a party.

The first bottles were opened, the glasses filled. The Padre explained that this was a very ordinary wine, good enough we must understand, but of no real dignity or importance. I translated what he said. The wine was last year's vintage. Second bottles were opened, and this it appeared was a much better wine, it had attained the age of four years. I felt my thoughts flying back to Luigi Costa and hoped that he had been away on holiday during the wine pressing. Third and fourth lots of bottles were opened, each a little older than the others, finally two bottles were produced and handled almost reverently. They were, the Padré announced, vintage wine, being no less than nine years old!

The party ended, for I protested that with more wine we should all be *ubriaco*—intoxicated. Don Martino said gravely, "Signora, if I do not have to see my friends safely down the stairs, I know that I have failed in hospitality."

The parish was poor in those days, the cottas of the altar boys were very old almost past mending. Through the kindness of the clergy at Farm Street, I was sent a magnificent parcel of cottas and two very good cassocks. They may have seemed old to Farm Street, but to us here they appeared magnificent. Don Martino was delighted and thrilled.

He took the Memorial service for my Mother, who died in England, but who had been living with me for a year in Sirmione; he also took the Memorial service for my cousin Brian, who died in Leysin and had lived in Sirmione for nearly three years. On both occasions he was kind, and infinitely sympathetic. Brian had become a Catholic shortly before his death —poor boy, he was only thirty-two—and Don Martino's reference to this in his oration was both simple and deeply touching.

When my father died, among other things his gold hunter watch, a massive presentation affair, was sent to me. I asked the Padré to call and see me as I had something for him. He came, and I shall never forget his face when I gave him the watch. He held it in his hand and stared at it, then said almost gaspingly, "For me? It is—gold, signora! I never thought to have a gold watch! It is—impossible!"

He showed me his own watch, a huge thing of white metal like a Town Hall clock weighing, I imagine, nearly half a pound. His father—I think he said—had given it to him at his ordination.

From then he always wore two watches, and if anyone asked him the time—which privately I think he very much liked them to do—he produced both and carefully compared the time shown on each before he announced the *exact* time to his questioner.

He celebrated the fiftieth anniversary of his appointment as priest to the Parish of Sirmione, the village was be-flagged, posted with coloured streamers asking that blessing might pour upon him, and wishing him long life. There was a special High Mass, and congratulations poured in from all the district round about. He was very proud and happy, I think.

Unfortunately there was a certain section of the community who—if they did not actively dislike Don Martino—expressed the opinion that "the parish needs a younger man". Someone more "go-ahead", more "up-to-date", the Padré might be all right for the old people, for the fishermen, he played a very fine game of *bocce* (a kind of bowls at which Don Martino was particularly good). Also it was known that the Parish Priest of Sirmione was not actually smiled upon in high places. He himself had told me that the Bishop did not like him much.

A small village invariably possesses its own underground "grapevine", and rumours spread, and small discontents were voiced. The older people, the poorer people never said a word against their priest, and—to tell the truth there was actually nothing that anyone could say against him. Nothing tangible, but intangible whispers can assume alarming proportions until the air is noisy with them.

That Don Martino heard those whispers I don't doubt, for I fancied that his figure was less ample, that his shoulders had begun to stoop a little, and that there were new lines in his handsome face. Then he was taken ill, he had a stroke. Not a very serious one, except that all such things are serious, but although he walked a little more slowly, and one leg appeared to drag a little, it was scarcely noticeable.

Notice came from Verona that he was to be retired, and

that a new priest would be appointed immediately; as a matter of fact he was appointed already. Don Martino, Parish Priest of Sirmione for over fifty years was superannuated.

He told no one, made no farewell visits, took no official leave —two good and loyal friends of his called for him before the village had awakened, while the lake still lay grey in the light of the very early morning. His small possessions were packed and put in the car, and they drove off to his native lake-side town of Malcesine.

He gave no opportunities for hypocrites to wring his hand and express their sorrow at his departure. He had watched the children he had christened grow up, be confirmed by the Bishop while their parish priest announced their names, the names which he had given them at the font. He had officiated at their weddings, made his sincere—if badly delivered—speech of congratulation at their wedding feast, and as the wheel came full circle again, he had christened their children. His had been the hand which had administered the last comforts which Holy Church had to offer the dying, he had admitted them to the great society of Christian people, and seen many of them on their way to join all those who had "kept the Faith".

His friends left him at Malcesine, and a short time afterwards we heard that he had died.

I have written about Don Martino at considerable length not because he was a man of any particular or notable achievement. I imagine that his actual knowledge from a scholastic point of view was only just sufficient to qualify him for ordination. I doubt if he read very much, except those books which were part of his daily life—the Mass, the Bible and his daily office. He was shrewd as people who come from peasant stock are shrewd. He could not claim many of the characteristics attributed to the famous Father O'Flynn and most certainly none of the ability to "trim his sails" with which The Vicar of Bray was credited.

He liked the good things of life, no one enjoyed a well-chosen, well-cooked dinner better than Don Martino, he enjoyed good wine, he liked companionship and liked joining in the social life of his parishioners.

His sermons as I have said, were lamentable, and in them he did not attempt to propound arguments of any profundity. They were merely concerned with "faith and morals", simply dogmatic addresses, delivered very simply and without any attempt at oratorical fireworks.

Apart from the fact—and fact it undoubtedly was—that he was not popular with those in authority, I doubt if he would have ever been given preferment, I doubt if he ever wished for it. He was utterly content in his own parish, among his own people; he was at their disposal for any advice or help which he could give them, spiritual or temporal.

As several elderly people here, who had known him all their lives, said to me: "He was the kind of priest who was right—for us."

I never knew the church, and it is a large one, anything but full for High Mass on Sundays. True, the children did not always behave very well, and I have known Don Martino's voice ring with, "*Silenzio!*" if they grew too noisy.

As a spiritual adviser he was essentially kind, his advice was always very simple and direct, you never felt that you were taking too much of his time or that he was in the least bored by your problems. His admonishings in the Confessional were gentle and essentially kindly. The Italians have a word for what is literally bad—criminals for example are referred to as being *cattivo*, children who are naughty often almost beyond the limits of their elders' patience are *birichini*. Don Martino made you feel that you had been *birichino*, and that you must try your hardest never to behave in that way again.

Everything is changed now, the church has new benches, which are just as uncomfortable as the old ones, it has stained-glass windows with colours which alternate between making you blink your eyes and feeling sick. The priest's room is furnished comfortably—and why not?—he has a handsome desk, and a comfortable arm-chair, he is an energetic man who certainly does not do his weekly shopping in Desenzano market every Tuesday, returning by the steamer carrying two large shopping baskets bursting with vegetables, the odd chicken and other things destined for the kitchen. And after all why should he? We have some excellent shops in the village now.

I sometimes think if I were to walk down the Lower Road, in the early dusk I might see Don Martino coming towards me, reading his Office from his open Missal. He would raise his eyes from the page, see me, courteously raise his *berretta* and say in that sonorous voice of his, "*Rispetti!*" and return to his Office.

III

JAMES NORBURY

T HE afternoon was hot, and the noise of cars, footsteps on the almost burning pavements and voices in multitudinous languages united in a confused chorus, the resultant sounds mingling and floating up and through the open windows of the Toucan Club. The club was open on that afternoon for a private party, your membership card went for nothing unless you were also the possessor of a card of invitation from May and José Adair to the "At Home" which they give every year to welcome me on my return to England after my usual ten months' absence.

The room was packed, as it always is at these parties, for the two Adairs have an immense circle of friends, and those friends are drawn from practically every walk of life. A poet wrote of this Toucan Club, where this particular party was held, saying:

——famous authors, and actresses as well
Of publishers, producers or television belles.
You may talk of Sirmione, or the vales of Timbuktu
Of Yorkshire, or the Atlas, the Poles, or Katmandu . . .

It was just that kind of a party! There was Marie Burke, looking like a young edition of dear Dame Lilian Braithwaite, Ursula Bloom and her husband, "only here for a minute because the two dogs can't be left alone in the car" . . . Bryan Michie of T.W.W., whom I remember years ago playing Dame in pantomime at, I think, the Hippodrome, and who was the most handsome Dame I ever saw, Hugh Ross Williamson, novelist and playwright, Vanda Godsell, the television actress, Georgie Wood, another person who can never stay for long because he is always rushing off to fulfil another appointment. He embraces you warmly, tells you it is good to see you again, whips out a diary—and insists that you whip out yours—and makes a date then and there when you can meet, then looks at his wristwatch, exclaims that he is "late already", and dashes away. Joan Hurley and her husband, who beams with pleasure as he watches her shedding her wonderful smile on everyone, for she is as popular as her wonderful aunt, Marie Lloyd. A small woman with red-gold hair, if everyone doesn't know her they make it quite clear that they wish to, Bryan Michie sees her and booms, "I must kiss Sara!"—and does. And everywhere, with a word to everyone, were May and José Adair. They appeared to know miraculously when a glass needed replenishing, when someone was longing for another of the wonderful canapés which were rapidly being consumed. Into this gathering walked James Norbury, whom I was to find his friends call Roy, except Ursula Bloom who remains faithful to the name his parents gave him and addresses him as—James.

"Mickie, you must let me introduce Roy Norbury to you." I turned at the sound of José's voice and saw a man of medium height, broad-shouldered, with a short, neatly trimmed beard. He was wearing a while silk jacket, a white waistcoat embroidered in gold, a white shirt, I think, frilled, and a voluminous scarlet cloak decorated with silver thread. He made a startling and arresting figure.

We talked, he was amusing, and emanated a sort of kindly warmth. He seemed to know everyone, to like them all, and I felt instinctively that they liked him. He invited me to dine at his flat. He asked Sara Turner also. He would call for us and drive us there. The evening came and James Norbury arrived with his car. By that time I had discovered that he was known as "Knitting Norbury" and that he was the great knitting expert. In magazines—women's magazines—he tells people how to evolve those intricate patterns of knitting which make the most modest tray cloth look magnificent when used as a border, how to knit wonderful jerseys, cardigans of unbelievably elaborate patterns, tiny jackets, frocks, coats, and the like which are calculated to make any infant proud! He encourages people who have invented their own designs to send them to him, and if they attract him, he buys the patterns and uses them in one of the periodicals with which he is connected. Many women in England may not be able to tell you the surname of the Archbishop of Canterbury, but they will —seventy per cent at least—know the name of James Norbury. He has written books on the art of knitting, and is now at work preparing a history of knitting which he told me can be traced back to astonishingly early ages. He collects pictures. Most of them are essentially modern, and I can neither admire nor understand them. He reads widely, loves music, travels whenever his work allows, and—collects friends I imagine wherever he goes.

We went to his flat for dinner, and found it "up four pairs of stairs", and no lift. I have long passed "the brave days when we were twenty-one", and except that the dinner was excellent and the conversation never ceasing, I don't remember a great deal about it.

The following year James invited me to dinner again when I came to England, he told me in his letter that he had moved, that the flat was on the ground floor—and I accepted. The new flat was charming, and—no stairs. Sara Turner was also dining there, and after an exceedingly good dinner, with what I was told was excellent wine and some very amusing conversation I decided that I liked James very much indeed. I found myself wondering how he had come to be Knitting Norbury and what his background might be.

On this particular evening, when we were drinking our coffee, Sara Turner and James began to argue. Now I enjoy argument, it both amuses and stimulates me, but I dislike any argument to go on for longer than half an hour. After that

I begin to get bored with the whole thing, and like to say to my opponent, "I think that I see your point, and though I can't altogether agree with you, I—etc., etc." Honour is satisfied and we can go on to discuss the merits of dogs, the value of space travel, or the chance of unity among the Churches.

Both Sara and James regard argument as a kind of endurance test. You feel that they are trained to the last hair, that neither of them will yield an inch, and the fight will go a full twenty rounds without the slightest chance of a knockout being delivered by either.

The argument was about capital punishment. James disapproves, hates and loathes it, Sara regards it as a horrible necessity. Both are completely sincere, and both are ready to fight for their opinions until they are exhausted. The rest of you—listen. You are not encouraged to take any active part. You listen, and think regretfully of all the brilliant and telling remarks you could have voiced.

Once James asked for more coffee, and I prayed that his strength might be ebbing. "The minster clock had just struck two"—only it wasn't a minster but an exceedingly handsome clock on James's mantelpiece. I yawned, the loud, offensive yawn of a tiger in the zoo when bored by waiting for its dinner.

Common politeness demanded that James should ask, "Tired, Mickie?"

I replied firmly, "Yes, particularly of this bloody argument!" Someone laughed, the spell was broken, Sara powdered her nose, James drank a long-since-cold cup of coffee. We got into the car, thanked James prettily for a lovely evening. I fancy that his eyes looked a little heavy, but Sara was as fresh as paint.

"Good night, James," she said, ready to start the car. "A lovely evening—but you're wrong."

I felt that his arguments were wrong, but I felt that he was right to restrict his reply to, "Lovely of you to come! Bless you!"

I felt that I liked James Norbury very much.

JAMES NORBURY

I heard people talk about James Norbury, almost everyone seemed to know him and like him. My curiosity was whetted, but it was not until he came on a very brief visit to Sirmione that I was able to satisfy it. He was enthusiastic about the place, everything in Sirmione appeared to enchant him. He stayed at a hotel which I invariably recommend to those of my friends who like simple comfort, good food and courteous service. There are at least two more—considerably more—costly than the one where James stayed, and while they are both more elaborate only one of them has ever given me a meal which I have really enjoyed. James was delighted with his small hotel.

One evening we took him to the Vecchia Lugana, where they grill lake trout over an open wood fire, where everything is simple, beautifully clean and the service is good and—friendly. I thought that I had safely steered the conversation into calm waters, then a sudden unexpected current bore it into the danger zone of argument, and Sara and James sprang happily into the ring. James is a good Catholic, the type that is essentially happy in their faith, a person who is content to take certain mysteries as unexplicable—and leave them at that! Not gullible, able to hold decided and advanced views, but ready—in certain matters—to bring the light of modern reason to bear on the teaching of the Fathers.

Sara Turner was born, I imagine, with a brain—and a remarkably active and lively one it is too—which finds itself totally unable to accept any form of religion without proof. Saint Thomas ought to be her patron saint. She admits frankly her admiration for the Saviour, but cannot accept His divinity. She is completely honest, completely sincere. So on this particular evening "the sun went down and the stars shone out" and the verbal battle went on. Neither of them lost their tempers in the least; I sat making "animal noises" from time to time vainly attempting to press arguments of my own. They were still-born.

I ended it by insisting that even Signor and Signora Bazzoli needed sleep.

35

Sara said, "Poor souls, I expect they are tired—but James, can't you see that because of the miserable life, the wretched existence of the poor in the Middle Ages, it was necessary to——"

James, slightly breathless after a long explanation about the Spanish Inquisition, said, "Yes, it's getting late, but, Sara, can't I make it clear to you that the Inquisition was a matter of——"

I continued interpolating statements about the lateness of the hour, and finally delivered a verbal punch and—the thing ended.

The eyes of Denise Martin and Tony who were dining with us were bright like those of over-tired children sitting up too late, I was distinctly "feeling my age", Sara and James like birds waking to salute a new day!

The following day, I persuaded James to—talk about himself. His father was a blacksmith, at a time when the village blacksmith was not only able to shoe horses and do it exceedingly well, making the shoes himself, not "adapting" shoes turned out like ready-made footwear. He had a small farm, and even if his actual income was small, the family—there were several boys and girls as well as James—were always well fed and well cared for.

I can remember that type of small farm, run in conjunction with the tenants' actual business, the stock consisted of two or three cows, a multiplicity of hens of no particular strain, but good layers. There might be a couple of pigs, almost invariably the curing was done at home and there would be some hams, and a side or two of bacon hanging from the beams in the kitchen. There would be plenty of vegetables, no scarcity of potatoes, home-churned butter and altogether these families did very well indeed.

Money might not be plentiful, but food was abundant. James at the age of four was sent to a dame school. These schools were almost invariably kept by maiden ladies of middle age. Their own education had not been extensive and the

36

education which they gave their pupils was consequently limited.

James had already been taught to knit by his grandmother, for this was before the time of cinemas, radio and of course television was unheard of as yet. Therefore children were taught to knit as a means of providing idle hands with something to do and not leaving the job of amusement to Satan.

Punishment at school was given ungrudgingly, so James told me. If you learnt too slowly, you were caned for being idle and inattentive, if you learned too quickly, you were caned for "showing off" and "trying to be clever".

In due time James passed from the dame school to the village school, where "respectable men and women over eighteen able to read and write and make simple calculations" who were well conducted, were considered capable of imparting the rudiments of education to young children.

James's mother, possibly to augment the family income and to meet the cost of maintaining a growing family, became the village dressmaker. Apparently she was very clever at her work, and James says that he gained his first glimmering of the use of colour and design from watching his mother working on the dresses she was making.

He would leave the National School I imagine when he passed out of the Sixth Standard, and how he spent his time until he was sixteen he did not seem to remember very clearly. Probably he helped his father in the smithy, being a rural district no doubt he was hired by some farmer at hay-making and again at harvest. When he was sixteen, having never lost his interest in design, colour and knitting generally, he went to Paris. How much money he had to take with him I have no idea, but I know that in Paris he managed to live "the hard way". He told me that he literally swept and scrubbed his way into any of the great fashion houses where he could gain knowledge regarding the use of colour, design and form. It was hard work; many boys—for James was actually still a boy —would have given up the fight, but there was in his character

37

that grim determination which still exists in the British, particularly in the rural British who until a comparatively few years ago took immense—though unspoken—pride in their work, who were closely allied to the land. They watched their dreams materialize not by means of the films and television, and were not content to "make dreams their master".

So James scrubbed and swept, doubtless knew what cold and lack of comfort meant, lived sparingly and—watched and learned.

He made friends, useful friends, and among them Anny Blatt, who knew as much as anyone about knitting and the uses to which it could be put, the beautiful designs which could be made from wool, and the graceful forms which could be achieved by knitting.

When the Second World War broke upon the world, James already had his foot several rungs up the ladder, he was making a living which was losing its starkness and extreme poverty. He returned to England, and found himself unemployed. Once again life was far from easy. He lectured on knitting to the Women's Services, to Women's Institutes, designed one or two sweaters and cardigans for the various services, but he found life at that time not only difficult but frustrating. He wanted to climb to the higher rungs of his own particular ladder. He became a handicraft teacher in a school for problem children. He told me that he discovered during this time that there were no "problem children" only "problem parents".

The war ended, and here James talks of "my luck holding", though I feel inclined to quote a poem of Conan Doyle's:

> Don't tell me of luck,
> For its judgement and pluck,
> And a courage that never will shirk. . . .

He was engaged as designer by a firm in Manchester—L. Copley Smith. The chairman of the firm was a woman—Mrs. Dorothy Bird. Mrs. Bird must have been something of a talent spotter, for she saw potentialities in young Norbury, encouraged him in his work, fostered his ambition and became his very good personal friend. He remained with Copley Smith for a considerable time, and then was engaged as Chief Designer by the firm of Paton & Baldwins.

The firm made a wise choice in engaging him, and in them James found employers who were possessed of vision, who saw further than the covers of their ledgers and the details of their balance sheets. They made it possible for James to travel in search of new ideas, and new designs. Many of his designs have their origin in Australia, Africa, and the Near and Far East. He studied ancient paintings, wall pictures, native patterns and decorations and bore his sketches home to be adapted into knitting patterns. He is still given opportunity for research and assures me that knitting was known over two thousand years ago. It is perhaps not too much to say that James has played a great part in revolutionizing the "jumper". I can remember the time when they were hideous, shapeless things, which hung on the human body like a badly made sack, now they are accepted in all their modern elegance.

He talks very little about his actual work, if you approach the subject warily you may glean a few comments from him, and you realize that he has standards from which he will never deviate. He detests—ugliness. He loves colour, form and well-balanced and artistic designs. He has been called the Dior of Knitting, and this is more than a mere ticket, it is a description of the man's attitude towards his work.

I have always disliked the expression—a self-made man. Surely all men who have achieved anything worth achieving are self-made. True, there are people who are shot into ready-made positions and by either adaptability or sheer good luck manage to make a success, but in the main what we are we—make ourselves. Admittedly, James Norbury had good material to work on; ancestors who were straight dealing, honest craftsmen, and a mother who obviously possessed good taste and the love of form which her son inherited.

He had tenacity, determination and steadfastness. He knew

where his goal lay and allowed nothing to turn him from reaching it. He knew that, as Marie Lloyd used to say, "There's plenty of room at the top", and very early in life James decided that the "top" was more comfortable than remaining milling about with the crowds that push and jostle on the lower rungs of the ladder.

To-day he is established as the leading authority in his own particular branch of work, he has several books to his credit, a standard work on the art and history of knitting, and does a considerable amount of journalistic work.

He enjoys life—that is to say he appreciates all the good things that life can offer. He is selective as regards food and wine, and he never makes the mistake of asking too many people to his dinner parties, he chooses them so that like the food and wine which he offers them they may—mix harmoniously. His friends are multitudinous, for his taste in friendship is cosmopolitan, his enthusiasm for those friends is generous and unbounded. Should anyone prove malicious, unkind, or unreasonably touchy James is genuinely hurt, for at heart he is still a simple and uncomplicated person.

He is gay, loves to amuse and to be amused. He loves to show off his friends to the very best advantage. Although he is "a great talker" himself, I find that he prefers—conversation. The last time I dined at his flat before I left England, that delightful and witty person Douglas Byng was one of the guests, and I have rarely listened to better conversation in my life. It took me back to the days when real conversation existed, and did not rely on a series of "wise-cracks" culled from the latest American musicals.

At a party which is given every year for me on my return to England—it was at one of these parties I have mentioned before where I first met James Norbury—someone is always asked to make a little speech of welcome. Some of them have been kind but unquestionably dull, some of them have been short, charming and delightful. James was asked to make the speech of welcome this year.

He spoke, I suppose for four or five minutes; I have rarely heard a more polished speech, beautifully timed and delivered, and yet bearing the unmistakable sound of sincerity. So there are my impressions of James Norbury. Why many of his friends call him Roy I don't know, I have always intended to ask him but there have been so many things to talk about when we meet that I have always forgotten.

Admittedly this is a success story, a "local boy makes good", the story of a self-made man. Very well! I like to record successes, I am delighted when a local boy makes good and if James Norbury is "self-made", then what he has created is something very pleasant indeed.

IV

"BUSTER" LLOYD-JONES
William Llewellyn Lloyd-Jones

As I HAVE kept dogs, or rather as the majority of them have permitted me to call myself their "owner", when in actuality they owned me, I have had a long and varied experience of veterinary surgeons. Both in England and in Italy I have met them. I have met those who were obviously nervous of the dog they had been called in to treat, this applies particularly to Italian vets. They ask you what is wrong, stand a good yard away from the dog, and ask you to do the handling. This type are almost invariably very well dressed, have well-kept nails, are beautifully shaved and sometimes exude a pleasing smell of eau de Cologne. Dogs they may tolerate, for cats they have a profound contempt.

The second kind are the sort of man who says, "Dogs are all right, kept in their proper place. I've a dog, I'm very fond of him, but he knows better than to disobey me!" They handle your dog with large, rather coarse hands, if he shows his dislike of them they bawl at him, ordering him to "Keep still!" which, of course, the terrified dog proceeds not to do! These are the men who examine your very sick Peke and assure you that "a lot of it is put on, y'know. Pekes are like that, they're great fakers and love to have everyone running about in circles. Give him a good dose of castor oil."

I once ordered a vet out of my house for that piece of advice, refused to pay his bill, let him take me to the magistrates' court, where I protested that I could only afford to pay half a crown a week. The magistrate, who knew me, ordered me to pay that sum, which I did, until I was tired of the debt collector calling each week and paid the whole amount owing.

Then there are those men who are vets because there was nothing else in the world they wanted to be, nothing held any interest for them as a profession except the care and cure of animals, and without being in the least sentimental, they dedicated their lives to—animals. I have met two in England and three in Italy.

There are, no doubt, others—dedicated men and a few women—but I have not known them, but the five—one of them is no longer here to minister to suffering animals—the remaining four have long since qualified in my mind as—Beloved Physicians.

One of them is the man I am going to write about here. His name is Lloyd-Jones, but everyone calls him "Buster", though the name doesn't suit him in the least. He is no longer in active practice, for his health will not allow him to be, but he is still a "moving spirit" in an establishment in London under the guidance of a very charming and efficient woman, Miss Squire, who worked for and with Buster for many years and who now sells many of the excellent medicines made from Buster's prescriptions. Dogs may be washed and groomed there, and she considers any animal worthy of all the care and attention which she can give it; size, breed, social status mean nothing to her, any more than they do to Buster.

So that particular lamp originally lit by him, still burns very brightly. You can find it under the name of Denes, at 24 Holbein Place in London.

Now for the man himself, who was the originator of Denes Herbal Medicines. He is a medium-sized man, it is impossible to guess his age, indeed I have never tried, he looks essentially young. I have known him for many, many years and except that now the poor fellow is confined to a wheel chair, he looks exactly the same as he did then. His hair is so fair as to be almost white, his eyes are very bright, his skin remarkably clear and fresh looking. The chief impression which he made on me when I first met him was that he was infectiously gay, interested in everything and capable of tremendous depth of feeling about anything concerning which he felt deeply.

I was curious to know more about him, and after I had visited his kennels, watched his patients who were sufficiently well to "walk out", going for their constitutional in the charge of two kennel maids, my curiosity grew even stronger.

I knew that Buster worked incredibly hard, and it was obvious that he was not—and probably never had been—a robust fellow. I heard people talk about him, they would point to some much-loved dog or cat and say, "We've Buster to thank that he—or she—is still alive." I judged from various things he said when I grew to know him better that he was an exceedingly poor business man. I wasn't surprised, invariably those people who literally dedicate their lives to their work for others, never amass a fortune. I fancy that but for Buster's wonderfully devoted and loyal friend, Hal, and a certain secretary who worked for him he would have been in the bankruptcy court years ago!

As a child Buster lived in the country, in a house surrounded by a large garden. His first recollection of longing to cure sick animals he can remember when he was about four years old. He used to search the garden for that particular grass which he had watched his dog nibble with apparently beneficial results. He heard of ointments made from this or that herb and did his best to make it himself for his cats or dogs.

Without being sickeningly sentimental, he realized that his constant longing was to cure animals of whatever ills might attack them. The ambition coloured his whole childhood.

While he was still a small boy he contracted polio and was helpless for two years. From his bedroom window he could lie and watch the birds. When he saw them gathering in flocks round the elderberry trees, eating the berries greedily, he was delighted to hear someone say that elderberries contained iron, and that the birds were storing up iron to sustain them against the hard weather of winter and enable them to resist it.

44

Lying there, day after day, the little boy's mind worked hard. He evolved that firm belief that in their natural state all animals and birds must find the medicine they need. That medicine must obviously be found in the world through which they roamed and where they lived. Herbs, perhaps roots, even leaves and flower petals, these things must be the medicine which animals took when they felt they needed it. He remembered the birds clustering round the elderberry tree, his dog searching for some particular kind of grass, his cats seeking eagerly for some herb which they knew by instinct would be beneficial to their health.

That was how Denes Herbal Medicines began, that is why to-day, my Pekes are given pills made from seaweed, pills made from garlic, and why my canary pecks so greedily at a lettuce leaf!

The small, pale-faced boy with his shock of ash-blonde hair, lying on his couch, immobilized by illness, thought and thought hard. He realized his love for animals—and that included everything that moved and lived, large or small, wild or tame. More than that, he realized, too, that animals living in a domestic state were often ill, suffered dreadfully, and that often their sufferings were increased through the ignorance—and only too often by the indifference—of their owners. In his heart he felt a growing hatred of pain and suffering. People had doctors, there were chemists who would sell them medicines, there were hospitals—people were looked after quite well. The animals were another story!

Then this small boy decided on his own future—he would fight for animals, fight those giants Pain and Suffering. Like some child of the Middle Ages he was eager to join his Crusade. He grew stronger, was able to walk again, he went to school, though his health did not permit of his joining in games to any appreciable extent, and still he kept his goal before him. He read books about the treatment of animals in sickness, he studied animals themselves and whenever the opportunity offered did his utmost to help and protect them. He has told me how on nights when the rain poured down, the thought of cats wandering about, their fur soaked with rain, cold and possibly without homes or shelter, nearly drove him frantic with misery. In the huge gardens of his home there stood an empty cottage, intended doubtless for some married gardener or chauffeur. In the grate of this cottage he would make a splendid fire, there was always plenty of wood lying about among the trees. Then protected by a large umbrella he would set out to—find wandering cats. Every cat he saw he would catch and carry in his arms—no doubt the cat protested wildly, for in all probability it had a perfectly good home where its owners awaited its return with anxiety. To Buster they were all "lost cats" who were getting soaking wet in the rain, and must be rescued. He carried the cat back to the cottage, then went out in search of others. When he had collected what he considered to be a good amount of rescued animals, and when he, himself, was a good deal wetter than any of the cats, who by this time were lying very comfortably on sacks before a splendid fire, he brought them milk, and locked them in for the night.

As soon as daylight came, he went out to give the cats their freedom, and it was a source of lasting grief to him that none of them ever returned! That they all possessed good homes and returned gladly to their sorrowing owners never seemed to occur to Buster as a small boy.

When he was old enough to leave school, it was taken for granted that he would enter his father's—old-established and very successful business in the City. Buster felt that in common fairness he must give the idea a trial, and stood it for twelve months. Then he knew with complete certainty that he would never make even a reasonably good business man and told his father so. The statement that he wished to become a veterinary surgeon was received icily. There were arguments, endless discussions, recriminations, but the boy remained adamant.

He applied to one of the best known societies for animal protection, asking to be taken as a working student. He was

46

accepted, and his career began. Like all juniors in any profession he was given all the "dirty jobs". Where an office boy would have made tea, washed cups and ink-pots, he cleaned out kennels, cleared up after operations, prepared meals for the animals, and—was happy. He had his foot on the first rung of the ladder which would lead ultimately to his goal. Meanwhile he was watching, noting everything, and learning daily. He was sent to the various suburbs where the society had a branch, he worked from early morning until evening for a microscopic wage, and when he returned to the rooms where he lodged, he sat down to study until the hour was very late and he nearly fell asleep over his books.

He came to know London and Outer London very well—Putney, Balham, Wandsworth, Hammersmith, the East End, the Dockland district, and everywhere he found new experiences, gathered new knowledge, increased his skill and his understanding, and—was happy. He was never concerned with his own health, which all his life has been uniformly poor, only the health of his patients and their ultimate recovery caused him real concern.

He passed two of his examinations and was engaged as an assistant. Then followed years of very hard work, more studies, and at least sufficient time to develop his own particular theories more and more fully.

During the war years, because his health made it impossible for him to serve with the army, he went to the country, back to his old home and there in what might be called "make-shift" quarters opened a place where he might carry on his work. Probably not even Buster with all his enthusiasm and optimism bargained for the patients who were brought to him. People who had been evacuated from their homes in dangerous areas —though what areas did not come into that category in the First World War!—brought their animals to him, asking that he would "board" them. Animals who had been injured in air raids, animals so injured that the only thing left to do for them was to put an end to their pain kindly and painlessly.

The district where he had his establishment was itself in a pretty dangerous area, being in close proximity to one of the largest munition works in England. One evening he heard that unspeakable traitor, "Lord Haw-Haw" announce that the factory was due at the very first opportunity to be demolished by German bombers! There were numerous air-raids, and after each one Buster and his helpers would sally out to collect animals left wounded, possibly trapped in bombed houses, or even running distractedly about the country-side half crazy with fear. More and more animals came crowding to his kennels, there was scarcely room for them all—but somehow Buster managed to—make room.

It was then, I think, that he began that practice to which he adhered for the rest of his life as an animal physician. If there was not sufficient room, if an animal was critically ill, and possibly needed hourly attention, automatically it slept in Buster's own bedroom, so that he could be on the spot to give it the intensive care which was the only way its life might be saved.

Food was a grave problem, and he told me that his gratitude to those friends who would literally scout round to whatever shops sold meat for animal consumption, standing for hours in queues, or saving and scraping from their own meagre rations whatever they could spare and bringing it to him for his poor evacuees, is still unbounded.

The war ended, and he looked round for suitable premises for permanent kennels, satisfactory surroundings, and a house which was what he needed where he could make a home. He found the ideal place at Preston Park, Brighton. He named it Denes Close, and first canvassed all the people who lived near the place he had selected to find out their feelings and opinions about having a kennels so near to their own homes. Without exception they agreed whole-heartedly. A charming house exactly suited to his needs, sufficient land to make it possible to build modern and comfortable kennels, a hospital, maternity wards, an isolation ward—everything needed to make the place ready for his animal patients. Added to that a garden which he loved and which grew to be a thing of great beauty. Then began what was, I imagine, for Buster one of the happiest periods of his life. He had the joy of watching the garden emerge from being a wilderness to become a thing of beauty, there were great trees, plenty of grass where he could see his dogs and cats—for somehow animals under his care became friends and lived happily together—searching for those herbs which instinct told them were good for their health. There was an elderberry bush, where the birds could eat the berries storing up the iron they needed to defend them against the winter cold.

He was extending his preparations for using more and more herbs for his medicines, continually finding new herbs which had beneficial medicinal properties. Patients came flocking in, many of them brought from a hundred miles away. He had requests to go as far as two hundred miles to visit a sick animal —and he always went. I saw those kennels, saw Buster's operating theatre, saw the dogs' and cats' food being prepared, watched them being taken out for exercise, and I realized what a huge machine this man, in spite of the ill health which had dogged him all his life, had set in motion.

He was sent for by the directors of zoos and cheerfully and successfully treated any animal which needed his help. His patients included elephants, a porcupine—which grew so tame that it would follow him about, a tortoise with a broken jaw who was fed on a paste of lettuce and garlic and also followed Buster about like a dog—anything that lived and breathed needing his help was Buster's business! His own special friends, his intimate companions were his dog Jackie, and a Great Dane—I think her name was Gerda—a cat called Rapunzel, and Wanda the monkey. There was a parrot too for whom he had a particular affection.

He might have been, could have been—he would never say "should have been"—a very rich man, but we all know that the doctor—whether he attends humans or animals—is too often the last person to be paid. Then again, as Buster says, "There are many people who can't pay!" and if you have a heart like Buster's that fact is the last thing that would influence him when asked to treat an animal. Even the people who pay their bills promptly and very cheerfully, can't pay for the concentrated care and devoted nursing which their animal has been given. Again to quote Buster, "You can't put down hours of personal nursing, hours without sleep, in desperate cases practically hourly visits! How can you charge for those things —if you could, you wouldn't!"

His days were very long, it was no uncommon thing for him to be still working in the early hours of the morning. One day a week he went to London, and spent the day at Holbein Place, seeing patients, giving advice, having consultations. His luncheon—a plate of sandwiches and cups of coffee, his relaxation the drive back to Brighton, conscious that he had done a good day's work, and was entitled to drive without haste along the roads from which night had banished the congestion of the day, breathing the clean, fresh air, presently as he came nearer home, to be impregnated with the tang of the sea.

Even then, on arriving home there would be some grave case to visit, enquiries to be made concerning this or that patient, perhaps some bitch to help through a difficult whelping, and his engagements for the next day to be arranged with his invaluable secretary before he could get to bed.

Yet he loved it all, his only two regrets were that his health would not allow him to do more, and that the days were far too short.

In spite of his heavy work and long hours he remained always patient with his sick animals. He never bawled at them, his hands were always gentle and skilful no matter how nervous and difficult they might be. The people with whom he was angry were those who aroused his indignation.

A man came into his surgery one day with a very fine dog, I think that it was either a setter or a Great Dane, I forget. The man said to Buster, "I want you to bump him off for me."

Buster answered very coldly, "I have no idea what you mean."

"Get rid of him, put him down—I've moved into a flat and they won't have dogs there. Give him a dose of something—I don't know what you use."

"Is he ill? Suffering? Too old to enjoy his life any longer?"

"No, he's all right. I don't want him, can't keep him in a flat."

"What do you expect me to do?" I can imagine that Buster's voice came straight off the ice.

"I've told you! I want to get rid of him. Do what you like."

"I see. Now do you mind leaving my surgery as quickly as possible please?"

Buster kept the dog, it was a beautiful creature, and grew to love him dearly, an affection which he returned. Some months later when Buster was visiting his patients in the kennels, the dog at his heels, the original owner saw them and stopped.

"That my dog you've got there?" he asked.

Buster replied calmly, "No, it's mine."

"Isn't that the dog I brought to you to put down?"

"Bumped off, was I think your expression," Buster said very crisply; "you didn't want him, I did. He's my dog."

"I think I'd like to have him back. He looks wonderful. After all he was my dog."

With emphasis Buster said, "He—*was* your dog. He's mine now, you gave him to me to—do what I liked with. Now—" with a sudden burst of uncontrolled fury, "get out of my way. I'm busy!"

He moved away, the dog, who had recognized the former owner, and had lifted his lip displaying dangerous-looking teeth, followed Buster.

As his practice grew, as his success as a veterinary practitioner increased, his health declined. For years he had been obliged to go to France three times a year for specialist treatment. While there he made many friends, and while, of course—he was never able to practise professionally in France, he was

51

always ready to give advice, to voice his unshaken belief in his own herbal remedies and diets. One beautiful white poodle he treated while in France; she was covered with eczema and practically hairless through it. He suggested his remedies, the poodle's owners who were personal friends of Buster's were completely converted to his herbal treatment. The little dog recovered, and when she was shown at the most important show in France carried off the Championship of all France, the judges remarking in admiration at the beauty and thickness of her coat. Her daughter in her turn some years later also won the Championship and so did her grand-daughter when she in her turn entered the show ring.

I myself know of a beautiful poodle that was nearly driven mad with eczema, could not be left alone for a moment because she would literally tear herself to pieces and bite herself until she bled. I ventured to suggest consulting Miss Squire at Denes. She was treated with Buster's remedies, prescribed according to his suggested diet. She is now one of the most beautiful dogs imaginable, and not only well and healthy, with a splendid coat, but she is the admiration of everyone who sees her. She still goes—as many other much-loved dogs do—to Miss Squire for clipping and shampoos.

And Buster? The man who while still a little boy dedicated himself to the service of animals, who sacrificed himself for them, who fought his own illness to help animals to recover from theirs. As I said, his fame as a veterinary practitioner grew, he was sought after as a judge at the most important shows in the British Isles, they even asked for him on the Continent.

He tried to find health for himself, so that he might continue his work, the work which he loved. He went abroad for treatment, going in search of the sunshine which he was told might be beneficial. He and his friends hoped against hope, until it became obvious that he could carry on his work no longer. The practice had to be given up, the consulting rooms at Holbein Place transferred to the complete charge of Miss

Squire, though Buster is still ready to give advice if asked and consulted. He will even occasionally see a dog if one is brought to him by a friend seeking his help. He is—on the retired list. He spends his life in a wheelchair, surrounded by the friends who love him and admire all that he has done.

He has been a vegetarian ever since as a small boy he decided that he could not eat a chicken which he had seen running about, and had, perhaps, actually fed and watched grow from a tiny ball of fluff just having left the protecting egg.

He tells an amusing story of one Christmas Day when he had given all his assistants, his secretary and his domestic staff permission to go and spend Christmas with their own friends. He would manage. They assured him that they had left everything he could want to eat ready and in the refrigerator.

He had been busy all day, feeding the various patients in his own kennels—dogs, cats, and all the other miscellaneous small beasts which had been brought to him to receive treatment. He had paid several calls on other patients, and returned home very tired. And hungry!

He went to the "frig" and opened the door. There to his horror was a large and beautifully cooked turkey! He slammed the door, and made his Christmas dinner from bread and butter and cheese. He admits that he felt badly-used and pitied himself deeply!

The following day his staff returned, they met him smiling and expectant. "Did you enjoy your Christmas dinner? Wasn't it a beautiful turkey! We took such pains over it."

Buster stared at them, hurt indignation written on his face. They explained. They had made the turkey, a paste of nuts, vegetables and other ingredients of a vegetarian nature, and the model was exact and perfectly realistic. Whether Buster finally ate the manufactured turkey or not I do not know.

There is another aspect of this man, an aspect which I have never actually discussed with him but which he has referred to as also has his friend, Hal Higgs. I don't know whether either of them follow any definite religion, I do know that they are the last people I should imagine were introspective, though most certainly Buster possesses a vivid and active imagination.

He and Hal both told me that when Buster was working harder than most men who enjoyed perfect health, he was convinced that some Power was giving him help and the necessary strength to go on with his almost superhuman efforts, day after day. He added that now he has definitely ceased his active work, he feels that this Power has been withdrawn as if he needed it no longer.

He sits in his wheelchair looking out of the wide window in the penthouse where he lives and watches the dogs—some of whom he recognizes as one-time patients of his, galloping about, enjoying themselves and revelling in the fact of—being alive. He watches the people too, and tells me that he often finds them even more amusing than the dogs!

He is essentially cheerful, his friends—and he has dozens—come to see him, he is interested in their doings and in no way is his attitude towards life that of a saddened and disappointed invalid.

He had done what he decided to do from the time when he was a little boy, he has relieved suffering, achieved cures, given care and unremitting attention and affection to his patients, and he has seen those remedies in which he believes so firmly, established and accepted as a great contribution to the health of the animal world.

He is no disgruntled invalid, regarding life as a burden and making the life of everyone with whom he comes in contact, a burden too. So, I, who love animals, who have in my own small and insignificant way fought for them and the rights which I believe are theirs, have tried to pay tribute to a man who reached his goal, who played a magnificent game, and who now can look back on a life which held fulfilment. I am proud to be able to count myself—one of his friends.

V

BRYAN MICHIE

H E IS ONE of those people whom you feel that you have known all your life; yet when you come to try to pin yourself down to dates, you realize that in the first place he is far younger than you are, and in the second place there are years and years in which he played no part at all in your life. Certainly the years have dealt tenderly with him, for he looks and sounds exactly as he did when I first knew him— whenever that was.

He is a tall, rather heavily built man, with fair hair which holds more than a trace of red in it. I suppose you would say that his face is fresh coloured, though I am never quite certain what that means. His eyes are blue, and always ready to crinkle at the corners, and shine with good humour and amusement. His voice, which is lighter than you might expect from so big a man, is one of the warmest and kindest I have ever known.

If he does not really mean all the pleasant things he says to you, then he is one of the world's best actors, for they seem to bring the ring of sincerity. When that sincerity is coupled with his wide, spontaneous smile, well, the world seems a nicer, warmer and infinitely more pleasant place.

He must have a "hard streak" in him somewhere, or he could never have reached his present position, or have held the various positions which he has held with such success. However if there is "an iron hand" lurking somewhere, Michie must have practically cornered the world's supply of velvet gloves, for it is never apparent.

His father was an Aberdonian Scot who followed the calling of a house agent. He was strict, rigid, and regarded the stage and everything appertaining to it, as pernicious. His mother, for whom I gather Bryan had a very great affection, was a sweet-natured, easy going Irish woman from Galway. It is a remarkable fact that so many women of that type, sweet, rather gentle, and not given to allowing life and its burdens to lie over heavily on them marry men who, strictly upright, holding rigid principles, are inclined to see danger in even the simple pleasures which life offers.

Bryan was born at the village of Tichborne in January 1906. I don't know if there were many other children in the family, I know that Bryan has two sisters, who I am told are charming, rather quiet and have a great affection for their brother. At least someone told me about those sisters, and I hope that they really exist for they sounded delightful.

As a child Bryan lived and dreamed of the theatre. He longed to grow up so that he might go on the stage, and one of his earliest recollections is of himself standing on his father's billiard table, reciting that melancholy poem *Lucy Grey* to an invisible audience and reducing himself to floods of tears by his own dramatic powers. His father disapproved of this form of amusement for which his son had such a taste, and also I imagine expressed his dislike of the little boy's boots on the "board of green cloth".

So stern and consistent was the elder Michie's denunciation of the stage that he decided firmly that his son should become a schoolmaster. To that end Bryan had the final touches put to his education at the University of London. At the age of twenty-one he became a master in a boys' school.

The choice of profession was, Bryan assures me, a dismal failure. He was completely unable to keep any order in his class, and I know how true it is, that once you realize that you cannot keep order—which in common fairness to the children often means that you cannot hold their interest, and the children have probably realized that fact quite a considerable time before you—you might as well admit that—the game is up, and retire as quickly and gracefully as possible. His career cannot have lasted very long, for he says that in 1929 he saw an advertisement in a daily paper that Basil Dean wanted young men—"young actors", and Michie had never acted in his life—for a stage version of *Beau Geste* to be produced at His Majesty's Theatre.

Michie made his way to Basil Dean's office, there was a considerable crowd of young actors waiting for interviews, Michie had literally to fight his way through them. What excuses he made for pushing aside young men who probably actually possessed some small stage experience, I cannot imagine. He did it, and stood before Basil Dean. Dean looked him up and down, then said in that sharp incisive voice of his, "Yes, you'll do for the little Dutch Boy. Next!"

He was engaged! He was on the stage! He walked away treading on air, scarcely able to believe that his dreams had come true. Then came the moment when he had to break the news to his father. I should like to have the details of that scene. The father, giving a creditable imitation of the granite from his own native city, the mother hovering near, torn between pride in the future which she doubtless saw destined for her son, and anxiety as to "what your father will say". The father did not say a great deal, but doubtless it was very much to the point, then such was his disgust, suppressed fury, and consternation that—he fainted!

However, Bryan stuck to his guns, rehearsed, and doubtless felt the rough side of the producer's tongue at rehearsals, but his name was on the theatre bills, and he was an actor. *Beau Geste* ran for five weeks, then Michie was out of work. He found work, with a not-too-brilliant repertory company in Swanage for the summer season. He could have had no idea what life in a small repertory company was like. The salary must have been painfully small, there was the usual change of play every week. A week's rehearsal for a play, the production on the Monday, and on Tuesday morning rehearsals began again for the new play. Gruelling work, and offering no time to polish lines, or to evolve characteristics which would enhance the character portrayed. No wonder that the majority of productions given by the smaller and less gifted actors in repertory are dull and mechanical, or that the actors themselves develop what are called "repertory tricks"! Only people with unbounded enthusiasm or real talent can emerge unscathed so far as their acting is concerned. There are, of course, many benefits to be gained from repertory, it certainly trains the memory to receive new lines, though I should imagine that they fade fairly quickly from the memory once the week's production is over. Here and there repertory companies have a producer, young, energetic, with ideas and the ability to impart them to others. But they are rare birds, and found only too seldom.

Bryan Michie's comment about the time he spent in repertory, which was one season only, is that he was as bad an actor as he had been a schoolmaster. As a matter of fact he possessed a considerable amount of acting ability but he had to find his medium, and a good many years were to pass and a considerable distance covered on the long road to success before he found it. Out of work, feeling depressed and probably disheartened, he returned to London. There he met that great comedienne, Hermione Gingold, who was with Eric Mashwitz to whom she was then married. They were good friends to Michie, were interested in the young man struggling to make his way in the theatre.

They obtained for him a post as "effects boy" at the B.B.C. During the time when he held this position, it was his duty to demonstrate sound effects to distinguished visitors. Two of them were King George accompanied by Queen Mary. Bryan had to show off all his battery of effects. He rattled the thunder sheet, and announced, "Thunder, your Majesties." He manipulated empty cocoa-nut shells on a table, and beaming—few people can beam so engagingly as Bryan Michie—informed the listening royalties, "Horses' hooves, sire." Leaping into a box partly filled with gravel and tramping about in it, he said, "Marching feet, your Majesties." This kind of thing continued until he had run the whole gamut of the effects, and the King and Queen turned to leave to see some other department where the secrets of the radio would be demonstrated and disclosed to them.

When Queen Mary reached the door, she turned back and returned to where Michie was standing gazing respectfully at his King and Queen as they made their exit. Queen Mary came up to him as he stood staring, and said, "Thank you very much."

Michie was so staggered at this unexpected piece of graciousness, he was almost overcome. He forgot that she was the Queen of England, she was, to him, at that moment simply a very charming, kindly and delightful woman. He gasped, then said with real sincerity, "Thank YOU, my dear."

He says that there was complete horror depicted on the faces of all the B.B.C. officials, and on the faces of the royal suite, the person who remained smiling unaffectedly and warmly— and possibly partially through amused surprise—was Queen Mary.

Michie remained with the B.B.C. for ten years and rose to be Compère and Producer. The *Daily Express* organized a competition to discover which was the most popular voice on the B.B.C. Michie was voted the first favourite.

Personally I don't find that surprising, for his voice has a quality which is wonderfully warm. It expresses the character of the man himself! There are no tortured affectations, no "new and novel" pronunciations, no dragging in sentences of words of pompous Latin derivation when simple, everyday words would be just as telling, in fact far more effective. You never feel that he assumes a voice of almost impossible and certainly improbable refinement in order to impress. It was— and is—a natural, sincere voice, the words come with admirable clarity and are enunciated without giving the impression that the speaker is either choking from the presence of a ripe plum in the gullet or in difficulties with an exceedingly sticky caramel.

In 1936, Michie met Jack Hylton who sent him on tour with his own show, *Secrets of the B.B.C.* It ran for a year with considerable success and during that time Michie conceived a warm admiration for and a friendship with Jack Hylton which has lasted through the years. Bryan can and does wax almost eulogistic about Jack Hylton. He says, "He is brilliant, full of ideas that are ideas, not pipe-dreams pinched from someone else and fobbed off as his own. His love for the theatre, in fact for any kind of show business, is utterly sincere and very deep. Serious about work, but quite capable of throwing himself whole-heartedly into enjoying a good time, forgetting work and immersing himself in company with his friends. And of those he has and always will have—an army!"

He was steadily working his way up to the higher branches of the B.B.C. He did the interviews in *In Town To-night*, toured the halls, and also appeared on radio in that very popular show, *Youth takes a Bow.*

He enjoyed, as he said, "Looking for gold", and was responsible for "discovering" quite a number of young people who later made their way to stardom. Hughie Green, Morecambe and Wise, Johnny Lockwood to name a few of them; young, aspiring to reach fame as entertainers, and encouraged by Bryan Michie's own enthusiasm for anything which concerned entertainment.

That is one of the secrets of his success, he is *interested* in people and their work. Not only regarding them as potential successes, but just as men and women, boys and girls. The dilettante "I'm just doing this for fun" type arouses no interest in him, but when he meets individuals who are serious about their work, who don't imagine that because they are young, they know everything there is to know, then his interest becomes intense, and he will go to endless trouble to bring success nearer the grasp of these aspirants.

He toured the provinces, making friends everywhere. In the same company as his *Youth takes a Bow*, were those three brilliant sisters of Marie Lloyd, two of them at least scarcely less famous than their sister Marie. Alice Lloyd, Daisy Wood, and Rosie Lloyd. Talking to Bryan about them, for they were all good friends of mine, he spoke of them all with real affection.

"There was a great deal to learn from any of that family," he said, "and I was like a dry sponge, absorbing everything they could teach me. And how much it was! Alice, who at nearly seventy looked about fifty, she'd been a star in America, as big a star as Marie was in England. Daisy was a wonderful artiste as a single turn and a most adorable principal-boy. Rosie could sing a ballad as well as anyone I ever heard. Artists all of them, but what I loved best about them was their— humanity. They loved life, people, their work and somehow it 'came over' when they were on the stage. Microphones were their pet aversion! I've seen Alice standing at the side of the stage ready to make her entrance, suddenly spot a 'mike' on the stage. She'd turn to the stage manager, 'Take that thing off, please. We don't use them!' They were—were—" he fumbled for a word, then his beaming smile broke out, "They were just—poppets! All of them."

In 1940 Bryan played Dame in pantomime at the Palace Theatre. There was a fine cast, Florence Desmond, Arthur Askey and Eddie Gray. Bryan was one of the best Dames I have ever seen, not a great comedian, but a completely credible Dame. He was always immaculately clean, never wearing those "moth-eaten" old bits of fur and comic hats which so many comedians in pantomime used to affect; and so often their "wise-cracks" were as moth-eaten as their furs! In the Palace Scene, which was always the epitome of gorgeousness, he looked superb! Wearing an elaborately dressed wig and a gown of "more than Oriental splendour", he sailed down the traditionally wide and impressive staircase of the Palace Scene looking "a million dollars".

Part of this story is lost in the mists of time, but one day after the matinée the whole cast of the pantomime, in their Palace Scene costumes came to the Cinema at Marble-Arch to attend some function organized by the W.R.N.S. What the function was in aid of, I have forgotten, and why I was there in some official capacity I have forgotten also. I was standing talking to Dame Vera Laughton Matthews, the head of the W.R.N.S., when the taxis drove up and discharged the artistes from the Palace Theatre. Dame Vera Laughton Matthews's eyes were riveted on Bryan Michie as he sailed forward majestically.

"Who is that?" she asked me in an awestruck whisper.

I replied, "The Dame."

I introduced Florence Desmond, Arthur Askey, Eddie Gray and various others in the cast, Dame Vera Laughton Matthews was charming to them all. It was Bryan's turn, she turned to me and this time her whisper was almost agonized in its intensity.

"Do I say 'Dame'? Is he—or she—a man or a woman?"

"A man," I said, "I'll introduce him by his proper name, Bryan Michie," which I proceeded to do; Bryan smiled delightfully, murmured something and passed on. The real Dame's eyes followed him. She said, "She's remarkably handsome, isn't he?"

He has played in eight pantomimes in all, and once when I think the pantomime was *Cinderella* at the King's Theatre at Hammersmith, he met me with Georgie Wood. Bryan was full of excitement. "I'm going to play one of the Ugly Sisters at Hammersmith! Would you like to play the other?"

Would I! When I was younger one of my dreams had been to play principal boy; as I realized that the years were passing, that dream had to be abandoned and I visualized myself as "One of the Uglies". Before I could give my excited reply in the affirmative, George's rather clipped, incisive voice cut in, "Certainly not! No to both of you, Mickie's most unsuitable!"

It is characteristic of George Wood that we both accepted his decision without a murmur. So the second of my pantomime dreams faded. If anyone asks Bryan Michie what his ambitions are, he always says, "One of them is to play one of the Ugly Sisters with Naomi Jacob playing the other."

By this time Bryan had reached the "Big Brass" type of

position in the B.B.C. He was the second person to compère *Housewives' Choice*, which ran for years. Then in 1950 Jack Hylton sent him as his representative to the United States. There he was responsible for bringing over a number of musical shows—*Kismet, Pal Joey, Paint Your Wagon, Wonderful Town* and others. He remained in U.S.A. for nearly six years and came back to go into television. When T.W.W. began in 1957, he became Programme Controller, which position he still holds with great success. Incidentally Bryan gave me my first chance to appear in television.

He was unable to get down to Cardiff for the production, though he was there to meet me, to dine with Sir David Llewellyn, and then dash back to London. However, the moment my appearance was over, there was Michie on the long-distance telephone to tell me, "Went over fine! I'm delighted!"

That is typical of the man, no matter how busy he is, how many calls he has on his time, he *makes* time to do a thing of that kind to reassure someone he knew had been nervous of their first appearance on television.

He was given the work of meeting important people who came to the old Savoy Hill Broadcasting H.Q., I should imagine because Bryan's cheerful calm, and innate friendliness put people at their ease before they had to "go on the air".

One of the V.I.P.s who was placed in his charge was that great actress and wonderful woman, Dame Madge Kendal. Now, great woman though she undoubtedly was, Dame Madge Kendal could be a very difficult person. I have seen her "in action", in a film studio where she had come at the invitation of Seymour Hicks to see "how films are made". After vowing that she refused to have herself filmed, which no one had at that juncture asked her to do, she agreed to have a few feet of films taken of her. No leading lady, no prima donna could have been more insistent that everything should be exactly— and "exactly" is the operative word!—as she wanted it.

However, to get back to Savoy Hill and Bryan Michie.

Dame Madge arrived to take part in a programme which was to be a tribute to the memory of Sir Henry Irving.

Dame Madge stood firmly before the microphone, her bonnet of violet velvet looked, to Michie, somehow to be held at an angle which was a challenge in itself. He asked if she would take off her gloves, otherwise it made it difficult for her to turn the pages of her script. She replied, very coldly, that she most emphatically would not remove her gloves. When the time came to turn the page she could not accomplish it—still wearing gloves! Again she refused to remove them, announced that she would not and could not do the programme and, turning smartly, left the building.

Lady Tree was telephoned for, and fortunately was able to come at once and "take over".

Later Bryan discovered that Dame Madge was nursing a grudge against the B.B.C. They had bought her house in Portland Place for which she had a great affection; it was necessary for the extension of what is now Broadcasting House. She nursed it and the fact that she had to vacate the house as a grudge, and also regarded the purchase as a personal affront to herself.

A great lady, a magnificent actress, but "difficult". Years ago Bryan and I both went to the same dentist, and a very excellent and successful dentist he was too. Both of us had a great affection for him. He disliked "meddling" with your teeth and one of his favourite precepts was "Let sleeping dogs lie". So unless a tooth was giving you agonizing pain or showed some obvious signs of decay, his comment almost invariably was, "Ah, yes, well my advice is let sleeping dogs lie." Michie and I met one day and were discussing our respective and recent visits to this dentist.

Michie said, doubtfully and regretfully, "You know I believe that my mouth is full of sleeping dogs lying!"

I asked him to jot down a few notes for me when I proposed to include him in this book; I wanted a list of the people he had met and his brief impressions of them. The list came by return of post, but apparently Bryan has met no one he didn't like and for whom he had not a great admiration. Reading through what he had written I found that I agreed with him in practically every case but what, knowing the man as I do, I realized was that what he had written is all no less than the exact truth.

Probably there are very few people he does not like and that is in no small measure due to himself. He does "make you feel good", he raises you in your own estimation, you feel that you are able to be amusing, that you are a highly intelligent person and the most satisfying part of it all is that you feel that Bryan Michie feels that you really are all those things!

That, I am convinced, is one of the reasons for his success. He likes the people who work for him and with him, he is convinced that they will always do their best, that they will "give him a square deal" as he is prepared to give them.

"We needs must love the highest when we see it", and Michie believes that he has found the highest, and in consequence that is what he gets, the very best that particular person has to offer.

I have been in many studios, film, radio and television, some have been pure hell, others have been pleasant and delightful. I have known producers who were ineffectual, brutal, carping, and others who stand out in my memory as having really helped the artistes they were producing, who have been reasonable, logical and considerate. Looking back—and I can look back over a very long stretch of years—I have never found studios where a more pleasant, friendly atmosphere exists than at Bristol and Cardiff under the auspices of the T.W.W. I have never met personnel who were more courteous, anxious for the comfort of artistes, more sparing of criticism and more generous with their praise. Those qualities which I have found in the Controller of Programmes, Bryan Michie, are demonstrated by every member of his considerable staff, from the producers to the waitress in the canteen, and the commissionaire at the gate.

You are not a servant of the organization paid, and paid very well, to deliver certain goods which must be up to a required standard; you are treated as an honoured guest whose visit is a pleasure to everyone concerned.

You do deliver the goods, you try to make them as satisfactory as lies in your power, in short, you want to please the people who try so hard to please you and put you at your ease.

That may seem to have wandered a long way from Bryan Michie, but I hope anyone who reads this will see the point which I am trying to make.

So there he is, that big, broad-shouldered, kindly man who has "come up the hard way", and still retained his zest for life, and his belief in the essential decency of a large percentage of the people with whom he comes in contact. He is still considerably younger than his actual years. You can work out his age for I have given the date of his birth at the beginning of this chapter. I have just worked it out on a bit of paper for myself, because I wanted visible proof and even now I find it very hard to believe.

On his journey through life, he has "ta'n a firm, firm grip o' the heather", and the journey has gone very well. That Scottish tenacity, and his Irish ability to smile easily have stood him in very good stead. Many years ago a rather unimportant music hall artiste managed to get an interview with a very important agent. The great man looked at the little one.

"What are you?"

"A comedian."

"Comedian, eh?" then grimly, "Make me laugh".

Bryan Michie would have succeeded in doing so!

VI

CECIL ROBERTS

A WOMAN friend of mine was glancing at the books on my shelves in the study. They are untidy shelves, because there is never sufficient room in them for all my books. There was originally, for I have told before how I came out to live in Italy bringing with me only seven books. True, I left a considerable number in store with my furniture, and gave a good many to John Ellison—that clever young man whose ambition was to write plays and who is one of the important figures now in the B.B.C. In those days he was running a book-shop, and I fancy that he had as little money as I had. I gave him my surplus books to start his "second-hand department". I don't fancy that the venture was a great success, though I may be wrong. The next time I met him he was doing that item called *In Town To-night*. We only meet nowadays by chance when I am at Broadcasting House, when we embrace fervently, promise to meet again very soon—and never succeed in doing so.

However, let me get back to the shelves in my study. There are books which you simply have to buy, they are a distinct "must", and so my shelves get more and more crowded, and more and more untidy. I occasionally give away a few—in misguided bursts of generosity, and always regret it!

So on this fine day, my friend was looking at my books and found a number bearing the name Cecil Roberts.

She said, "He's done very well, hasn't he? To have started as a railway porter at Victoria Station."

"Railway porter—nothing!" I said, "I've heard people say that he is the son of a coal miner, but the railway porter is a new one on me. I'll tell you the true story of Cecil Roberts, because I know him."

I told the story which I am going to tell you. Let me say first that I admire his work, I admire his ability to give you information without ever becoming—informative, and in addition I am very fond of him, and I have a considerable amount of envy in my heart concerning him. I like him because he is a very pleasant, civilized person, I envy him because he can write much better than I can or shall ever be able to write.

I used to think when I met him what a pity it was that a young man as he obviously was, should have lost so much of his hair. As a matter of fact he isn't—a young man, but he most certainly isn't an old one! I doubt if he ever will be that because his mind and his general outlook on life are so astonishingly young. So when you meet him your impression is of a "young-ish" man, fairly tall, very very bright eyes which see with remarkable clarity, and twinkle readily. He has a clean-shaven, unlined face, a good straight nose, a mouth which is modelled in generous curves, and he is the possessor of a very clear and musical voice. That of course tells you precisely nothing, and you will find—if you have read his books—far more about what he really is than I can possibly tell you in a description such as I have just attempted.

His novels have great charm, they are not "slices of life" because that term has come to mean "Chunks of the nastiest side of life" and too often does not succeed in doing even that particularly well. Cecil's books sell enormously—even his early novels are still selling in considerable and most satisfactory quantities. Cecil Roberts is no "angry young man" longing to voice non-existent grievances and make a little money out of the wrongs, the injustices that have been done to him. He finds life a good business, he finds pleasant people interesting and sometimes amusing, and he has not found that the unfailing recipe for a good novel is a large number of prostitutes and an even larger slice of pornography.

His travel books are to me a sheer delight. They are not

heavy tomes containing facts and dusty historical references which may prove the author's erudition but are a damned bore to the average reader. His *And so to Rome, Portal to Paradise* and *And so to America* hold you captivated and bound to the book until you turn the last page and sigh because you have come to the end of it.

His poems were published two or three years ago—*Selected Poems*—by Messrs. Hutchinson. Some of them are almost heart-breakingly beautiful, and all are charming and well worth reading.

Now let me tell you the real story of this young man who admits to being over seventy—which I find strains my credulity considerably. It is a story of hard work, the story of another self-made man, except that he was born with an ability to write and take pains to write musically and with great charm. He developed, let us say, his natural talent, and at first it was— hard going.

His father fell dead in the street, leaving a wife and one son, Cecil. In those days there were no widows' pensions, no allowances for widows' children. The son was fifteen years old. He worked in a Government office and his wages were fifteen shillings a week. Not even in the "good old days" when you could rent a cottage—in a poor-class neighbourhood admittedly —for eight shillings a week could you live on the remaining seven shillings. The boy was clever, energetic and ambitious. Already he had learnt that there was money to be made out of writing articles which the public would like to read. He wrote them—he was paid on an average five shillings for each article, and that sum was most welcome and necessary to the family income.

The neighbourhood in which they lived was, Cecil admits, a very poor one, but with that possibly misguided, and probably rather snobbish, mentality which so often goes with the inability to live in the decent surroundings to which you have been accustomed, the mother and son "kept themselves to themselves". No doubt they were regarded as "stuck up", and equally no doubt that earned the rather sneaking respect of their neighbours. Even then, I expect, those same neighbours heard that "'e writes for t'paapers! Ondly sixteen mind you! Gets paid for what 'e writes too. Wunnerful 'ow 'e does it. No, I don't reckon they're all that badly off what wi' one thing an' anuther."

They certainly let half the small house off to a "remittance man", a gentleman and a scholar, brother of a clergyman who, I imagine, supplied the remittance. This new inhabitant of the Roberts' cottage realized that his landlady's son was an undeniably bright fellow and offered to teach him both Greek and Latin. Young Cecil, hungry for knowledge, jumped at the suggestion, and—hence his knowledge of both these languages.

He had other things for which to thank the fate which had sent the "remittance man" to their home. His brother lived in a fine old rectory with a splendid garden. When the rector went on holiday his brother went there to keep the garden in order during his absence. On these holidays he took his pupil with him and Cecil was delighted to escape from the noise and bustle of Nottingham and find himself able to breathe fresh, clear air, and enjoy to the full the space and freedom.

He looks back on those precious holidays with nostalgic affection, and when he wrote his first novel *Scissors* he introduced the old Leicestershire rectory in the book. That first novel was written in 1923, it is still selling and is now in its twenty-eighth edition.

He was sixteen when he invested sixpence in a second-hand book shop. I use the word investment advisedly, for like Cecil Roberts I can remember very well the days when if sixpence was available it was to spend on anything but actual necessities —soap, a tube of tooth-paste, even shoe laces or reels of cotton —and not squandered on books, even if they were second hand. Books might be necessities to us, we might actually prefer them to half a pound of tomatoes and a loaf of bread, but our stern common sense assured us that we were wrong.

However Cecil invested his sixpence and bought Hare's *Walks in Rome*. Now the estimable Hare is not the most lively travelling companion, but he does "tell you things". I have his Life Story, which he took six volumes to tell, and I have rarely read a duller set of books, illustrated by rather inefficient sketches of his own. However, his *Walks in Rome* fired young Roberts' imagination, and he promised himself that one day he, too, would walk in the Eternal City, and a great many other exciting and beautiful places as well. He had only very vague ideas as to how this promise was to be kept, but he had faith in himself and "never doubted clouds would break" and a path lie open before him. So when I read *Portal to Paradise*, I don't feel that Mr. Hare wasted his time since he first gave that determination to travel and to write of what he saw to Cecil Roberts.

So that was the beginning of what he himself calls a fairy tale and since then all kinds of things have happened. In 1960 the people of Alassio, where he had lived for many years, bestowed upon him the Honorary Citizenship of the town, and the ceremony was honoured by the presence of Britain's Ambassador to Italy. An Honorary Degree was awarded him by a famous university, his books are published in a dozen different countries, his sales in America vie with those in his native country. He has travelled, and not only travelled but knows intimately untold cities and the countries in which they are situated. Knows them sufficiently well to use them as the settings for his various novels and make you realize that the book is written by a man who knows the place, the country and the people who live there. I once knew a very successful novelist who wrote novels with a setting in most distant places —China was his wash-pot, and over Japan, Tibet, Afghanistan and Persia he had cast his shoe.

I said to him, "You must have travelled all over the world!"

"Never been out of Europe, then only Paris and the South of France, oh, I once went to Spain to get local colour for a bull fight. I was sick and disgraced myself. No, a shilling handbook tells you all that is necessary, that and a few coloured pictures give you all the information you need—if you have any imagination."

He scratched the top layer of the soil—Cecil Roberts sinks positive shafts and then goes on digging!

He does not restrict his characters to one particular class of society—they are neither uniformly exalted society, with stakes in the country and diminished bank balances, neither are they all pimps and prostitutes dwelling in the stews of some huge slum-filled city. His characters do not propound at length the author's political and religious opinions to which his friends would never listen in ordinary conversation but creep silently away, like the Arabs in the poem, and leave him to talk to the empty room. He rides no hobby-horses, and propounds no particular message to the world at large.

Yet, and as this is how I feel—a very ordinary person indeed —I feel that hundreds of other people must feel as I do. I am better for reading a novel by Cecil Roberts. His travel books fall into a different category of course. Those give you stimulation, rouse in you a longing to see the places of which he writes, and some day to claim the intimate knowledge of them which is so evidently his.

The novels are of real benefit to me. I finish them feeling happier, the women may be good—very good—and why not? I have known good women and so have you. His men are usually good-looking, which is no crime in itself, and after all is something not altogether unknown.

There are pleasant people in his books, people I at least like to know. If you say that an author writes about "nice" people, you are supposed to be adopting a slightly patronizing tone about his work. I am tired of reading about teenagers who could qualify as young criminals or budding sex maniacs, tired of thugs and swindlers—unless they are the engaging kind who went to a public school, carry unobtrusive gold cigarette cases, and have their clothes made in Savile Row, then I am snob enough to have a weakness for them. Crimes of violence frighten me, drug addicts bore me, crude sex on every page ad libitum and ad nauseam sends me to sleep, and I repeat that I like pleasant human people, with failings and frailties and clean necks and nails which have received attention within the last week or two at least.

I feel that Cecil Roberts had enjoyed writing about them, that he had done so without a wet towel bound about his brows, or shivering on the brink of a nervous break-down.

He tells a good, credible story, tells it in good English, and admits that he prides himself on his—integrity. He either knows his facts when he begins to write, or he goes to considerable pains to verify them. If he says that a train leaves Ashby-de-la-Zouch at 1.25 you can be sure that is the time that it really did leave on the date of which he is writing. That may be a very trifling thing to mention but if you happen to know that particular town and its train service, it is annoying to find that there is a train credited with leaving at 1.42. That integrity—of which I have given a small example—is all part of his work. It may all read so smoothly and be apparently easily written, but if you think for a moment you will realize that the "easy" English, the small often unnoticed facts, references to places, are all correct and imply a great deal more care and attention than might seem apparent at first sight.

I remember receiving an irate letter from some retired general, because I had made the British Expeditionary Force leave England four hours before the first battalions left in 1914. Cecil Roberts would never get a letter like that one—because he would never have made such a mistake!

They are the sort of books which make young people feel, "I wish it could all happen to me", and elderly people sigh and think, "How I wish all that might have happened to me when I was young."

Read—if you haven't done so already—*Scissors, Wide is the Horizon, Victoria Four-Thirty, They wanted to Live*—that is not a complete list for I am quoting from memory—and I feel certain that the feeling of happiness will make itself felt for you as it has done for me.

His travel books are vivid, and having read one of them you feel the impulse to put away your work and seize various guides, and books giving information as to hotel accommodation and set out to see what Cecil Roberts saw. Only if you are to see what he saw, then you must cultivate an "all seeing eye", you must set out as a Jack Hawkins, looking for gold, and you must possess a mind which is still curious, and a heart which is still young, eager and longing for the adventure of finding new beauties.

Perhaps in his poems you can find the real key to the man himself. I like to think that I did. He is at heart an incurable romantic. That does not mean, emphatically, that he is what was once described as "a greenery-yellowey, Grosvenor Gallery, foot-in-the-grave young man".

I imagine that all his life he has been greedy for knowledge, that whenever anything has fired his imagination he has wanted to know everything that was possible concerning it. I seem to remember many years ago he came to Sirmione when I had a man staying with me who was a building contractor. I have an idea that Cecil had recently built himself a cottage, or taken over some house which was almost derelict and restored it. Whichever it was, he and this man began talking about roofs and their construction. I have to admit that they both bored me, they got books and propped them up to make models of a roof, they argued, their eyes shone with pleasurable interest and they entirely forgot all about me. Then I heard words such as slates, tiles, thatch and gathered that they had moved on from the actual building of a roof to covering it. I felt that this new subject would prove inexhaustible, and rang for tea!

After Cecil left, my friend said to me, "Is he a builder?"

"Don't be silly, you know he's a writer."

"Yes, but I thought he might do that as a hobby, and that his real job was building. I'll swear that he knows more about it than I do."

You see, that's the kind of mind Cecil Roberts has! He could talk just as easily—and correctly—to a steel riveter, a carpenter or a trick cyclist. Much of it might be theoretical, but his theories would be completely convincing and founded on actual knowledge.

Some time ago I appeared in a television series called *Approach to*—— One of the interviews was with Dame Rebecca West—for whose work I have always had a profound admiration—and Paul Gallico. Both of them I felt, and both—remember—are excellent writers, did not seem to me to find their work wildly enjoyable or exciting. Now, Cecil Roberts does enjoy "telling a story", he admits it. He says, "All these books gave me great pleasure in the writing." He adds that he marvels sometimes that three generations of the public have been so consistently faithful!

Personally I see nothing to marvel at, I believe that the public are, taking them by and large, very shrewd, and very often completely capable of detecting what is false and what is true. They may accept these vague works, which have apparently no particular beginning and no obvious end, those books which meander along dealing with the neurotic types who are so unstable that the author can make them do and say—anything, for the simple reason that nothing they say or do bears the slightest resemblance to reality. They very soon see through the affectation, the blatant conceit, and the unforgiveable arrogance of these writers, and although they may have a brief vogue, and a restricted one, then—they disappear and are no more seen.

Cecil Roberts tells a story, it may not even be a very profound story, he may not face you with a new psychological problem on every other page, he may mention a kitchen sink, but it will be a perfectly clean and hygienic one and not used as "atmosphere". You read one of his good stories, you enjoy it as it is obvious that he has enjoyed telling it, you remember it with pleasure, and you wait for the next book he writes with happy expectancy.

75

Someone I know was extolling a book to me the other day. I had read it, it concerned a group of people with artistic "leanings"—though they never appeared to lean very far—who always drank "doubles", and mixed their drinks regardless of consequences. The consequences were most unpleasant. They appeared to prefer dirty sheets to clean ones, a number of most unpleasant homosexuals wandered on and off the scenes, there was a vivid description of an operation performed to induce an abortion, and the whole thing was like a dream after a dinner which was too heavy and induced complete indigestion.

My friend said, "There's a book for you—a book!"

I replied, being an uninhibited person, with one of those phrases which would have horrified our mothers, and which are accepted as common currency in modern conversation.

My friend snapped, "Could your friend Cecil Roberts have written a book like ——?" I don't give its name, who am I to advertise wares which don't please me!

I replied, "Of course he couldn't! It would bore him to extinction to even try to. He likes to enjoy writing!"

Cecil tells a story himself about one of these clever young men who set to work to explain the reason for his, Cecil's, success. He didn't deny the existence of that success, but he explained, with much delving into psychological jargon, that it was due to a certain cunning, the possession of a third-class mentality and also a great deal of—luck. Cecil listened in silence, allowing the waves of erudite brilliance to break over him. Then he said mildly, "You have forgotten one thing which has contributed to my success. I *can write*!" And there is the whole truth of the matter—he can write, and what is more he can write a story. There is a story in everything he writes —*And So to Bath, And So to Rome, And So to New York*—all of them are facts that have stories in which they are set.

I suppose that making your way by writing, perhaps by any means, can have several ultimate effects upon your character. I have known men who gained success the hard way who have become bitter and sour, they may enjoy the fruits of their success but they are cynical about it. Others who in their heart of hearts believe themselves to be very clever fellows, adopt a slightly sneering attitude to the position which they have attained, "scorning the ladder" by which they ascended. To the people they knew before they were crowned with the somewhat perishable laurels of success, they are either effusive to prove their generous, warm-hearted natures to whatever audience may be present, or exceedingly cold, and patronizing.

Cecil Roberts has come to his present position along the hard road, and I feel that there is in his make-up a certain delighted surprise that he has climbed the heights which he has reached. He doesn't allow it to be too apparent, he never stresses the fact that the five shillings he earned for his early articles were not only welcome but absolutely necessary to make his and his mother's lives possible. He doesn't tell you how often his boots had to be re-soled, or what cheap meals which were also very good, could be provided for sixpence, making his hearers desperately uncomfortable, and hot behind the ears.

He tells you that he stays at the Grand Hotel in Rome and adds with a contented smile that he pays as much in a week when he foots his hotel bill, as his mother and he lived on for a month. Tells it as if it were a delightful and amusing fact, and as a surprising fact which never quite ceases to astonish him.

Incidentally he was staying at the Grand during the time when the great gathering of eminent clergy was convened by the late Pope. Many of the exalted clergy stayed at the Grand Hotel, which has always been popular with famous divines, diplomats, and royal personages. On either side of Cecil's room were those occupied by a Bishop and a Cardinal, men of "credit and renown", and men who also appreciated the good things of life. Let me add very hastily—and why not?

Meeting his Eminence the Cardinal one morning in the corridor they stopped to pass the time of day.

Cecil told His Eminence that he had a Cardinal on one side and a Bishop on the other side of his room.

The Cardinal smiled, "You live in the odour of sanctity, Mr Roberts."

Cecil agreed. "Indeed, yes, your Eminence. I never realized before how strongly it is filled with the scent of good cigars."

The Cardinal was delighted and doubtless recounted the story to his brother cardinals, who probably in their turn recounted it as having been said to them. And again—why not?

So there are my impressions of the man; he enjoys life, he enjoys his success, extracts pleasure from his lecture tours in America where he is very popular both on the platform and to the reading public. So there is the story of another—self-made man! And as he said of himself, "*I can write*." He certainly can!

VII

SIR SEYMOUR HICKS

To me he will always remain—The Last of the Wits. There are still men who are amusing, even witty, but it is not the constant, effortless wit of Seymour Hicks. I have heard and read that many of the witticisms voiced by both Oscar Wilde and Sir Herbert Beerbohm Tree were carefully prepared, even rehearsed before they were uttered in public. They dropped them easily, with a nonchalant air; like pearls, they were something precious, worthy of preservation.

Seymour Hicks flung his witticisms in a wide arc as a woman scatters corn to feed her hens. He was completely prodigal! His sallies of wit were not regarded by him as being of great value; unlike the epigrams of many of the Victorian and Edwardian playwrights, you did not mentally see a road being carefully prepared for them, so that they should meet with no obstacle. They simply rose up like the bubbles in a glass of champagne, uncounted because they were countless.

I am not being particularly successful in conveying to people who never saw him or knew him what his wit was actually like. He was never that dreadful thing a "funny man", "a born comedian" when those expressions are applied to some tedious buffoon who is forever letting fly wise-cracks in and out of season. You never stood around—waiting for him to be amusing. His witticisms were completely unexpected, they came bringing no faint aroma of moth-balls, and they were never —dubious.

To-day I read of men and women who were accredited wits. My reading is punctuated by my groans. They may be silent groans, but they are very real. Some of us still remember the play *Charlie's Aunt*, in it one of the characters tells a story. A poor story admittedly. There is a polite titter from the other characters, except one young man who says firmly, "What a damned silly story."

How often do I mentally exclaim that when I read this kind of thing.

"I remember one particularly amusing evening. XYZ was in great form and kept us all in roars of laughter. Lord ABC said what a wretchedly wet day it had been. Quick as lightning XYZ said, with perfect gravity, 'Not nearly so wet as last Wednesday.' He was inimitable!"

And that is scarcely, if indeed at all, an exaggeration. Emphatically that was not the brand of humour which one came to look for from Seymour Hicks. First of all he was far too good a "trouper", and he would have scorned to inflict such arrant rubbish on his audiences, and secondly he was far too great a wit to find the slightest pleasure in indulging in such utter nonsense.

Now for the man himself. He was born in 1871, in Jersey. His father was a regular soldier, a captain in the 42nd Highlanders. He had retired through ill health. For twenty-five years he had been the only English officer in the 42nd—the celebrated Black Watch. The retired pay of a Captain, no matter how distinguished either his regiment or his achievements while serving with it, has never been notable for its size, and Captain Hicks, his wife, three sons and a daughter were forced to live lives which were distinctly limited by—strict economy.

Seymour was destined for the Army, and Seymour disliked the idea whole-heartedly. He had never been passionate where learning was concerned; like so many people possessing alert and very quick brains coupled with a lively imagination, he did not shine as a scholar. He was more often the despair than the delight of his teachers. From his very early years, he longed to be an actor, and as the years passed that longing grew to be a fixed determination. On leaving school he was sent to begin his business career, having failed signally in his preliminary examination which would have been the first step in a military career.

Speaking of this examination he said, "I went up for the examination with no anxiety whatever. I knew that I had not the faintest hope of passing it."

He was sent to London to begin his career as a business man. The opportunity to become "an officer and a gentleman" was beyond his scope. "It seemed possible," he said years later, "that I might conceivably be the one but not the two taken in conjunction."

He was to begin work in a wine merchant's office. The owner was a Frederick Toole, a nephew of the famous comedian, J. L. Toole. Young Hicks received no salary, but was given an allowance of one shilling and fourpence a day which was to pay for his fares to and from work, and his lunches. He remained with the wine-merchant for six weeks, hating every day of them, doing everything he could imagine to "get himself the sack". He achieved his desire, by signing bills of lading to get a large quantity of champagne out of bond, when the bills should have been made out for—port!

He announced that as he had failed for the Army, failed for the City, he intended to do what he had always longed to do —become an actor.

Seymour Hicks began to climb "the hard way". A friend heard that there might "be something" at the Grand Theatre, Islington. There among a crowd of shabby supers, all standing about hoping that they might be given the chance to earn a shilling a night as part of a crowd, peasants, soldiers or whatever happened to be needed in the play, a young man came over to Hicks and said, "I'm the prompter, my name is A. E. Matthews. You can start supering to-night, if you like." Did Seymour like! The doorway through which he longed to pass lay before him. He was an actor—or would be by the time evening came. Presently Matthews came over to the crowd of supers, holding a small pile of brown paper-covered books, asking, "Can any of you here speak lines?"

Scarcely were the words out of his mouth, when young Hicks almost shouted, "Yes, I can!" and A. E. Matthews said years later when both he and Seymour Hicks were established actors and equally established favourites:

"He almost snatched about nine of the 'small parts' out of my hands, determined, I imagine to play them all!"

As a matter of fact he was given the small part of a postman, and his first words as a professional actor were, "A letter here for Mrs. Drayton." He had to deliver the letter to Charles Warner, a very well-known actor in heavy dramatic roles. Seymour's salary was raised to ten shillings a week.

The Grand Theatre, Islington, was burnt to the ground in the early hours of the morning when Seymour had been enjoying his first appearances for about ten days. This was a calamity. "The owners of the theatre were insured against their loss," he wrote. "I wasn't insured against the loss of my ten shillings a week."

He managed to get employment at the Olympic Theatre in Wych Street. His salary was fifteen shillings a week, then because he persistently begged to be allowed to "go on the stage", he was made call boy, though still retaining his secretarial job. So there he was rich in his own estimation at least, with a weekly salary of twenty-five shillings a week.

So it went on, he was climbing slowly, there might be small set-backs, but so long as he was in work he enjoyed the life, every minute of it.

He was playing at the Princess's Theatre, in a play called *True Heart.* He had to take a message to the manager's office.

As he walked in Seymour Hicks heard a woman speaking. Her back was towards him, and he could only see the back of her head covered with most attractive fair curls. The voice entranced him, and he wished that she would turn round, feeling that if her face was in keeping with her charming and beautifully set head and her delightful figure—her face must be something "very special".

She turned and began to walk out followed by the manager.

82

For an instant their eyes met, and Seymour thought that they were the most lovely eyes he had ever seen; expressive and yet calm, shining with essential goodness and kindness. Instinctively he felt that a man could find comfort, encouragement, and loyalty from the woman with eyes like those which met his for a brief instant. He stared after her, he heard someone in the office say, when she was out of hearing, "Ellaline Terriss, Breesy Bill's daughter." "Breesy Bill"—William Terriss, the idol of the theatre going public! Seymour Hicks sighed, he was only a call boy, "passing rich" on thirty shillings a week. He was to carry that memory of Ellaline Terriss in his heart for a long time, he did not even see her again for five years.

Touring the provinces followed, there were ups and downs, disasters, difficulties, all of which in later years Seymour Hicks told in his own inimitable fashion, and in retrospect made them seem to have been merely humorous interludes.

Then Fate took a hand in the fortunes of young Hicks. Arthur Cecil saw him act when he was spending a holiday in the Isle of Wight. He saw that this enthusiastic, mercurial boy had tremendous possibilities. He visualized a future for him which would establish him in the front ranks of the acting profession. Arthur Cecil gave him a letter of recommendation to Arthur Chudleigh, then manager of the Court Theatre in London in partnership with Mrs. John Wood.

Immediately on arriving back in London, Seymour lost no time in making his way to the Court Theatre. He was very nervous and fully expected to meet a grim, hard-faced business man. Instead he found Arthur Chudleigh to be a smiling chubby-faced young man about twenty-eight, who greeted him in a most friendly fashion.

He had nothing to offer young Hicks at the moment, but he knew that Mr. and Mrs. Kendal were looking for a young actor to play boys' parts in the company which they were taking to America. He added, "And now, what about going out for a spot of lunch?" The luncheon was followed by an introduction to Mr. and Mrs. Kendal. That, Seymour Hicks always

83

contended, was the turning point of his career as an actor. He was engaged to play the boys' parts in the plays which they were taking to America. His salary was to be six pounds a week, with a rise to eight pounds a week should he remain with them for a second year.

Probably no young man could have entered a better school, for Mrs. Kendal—Dame Madge Kendal as she was destined to become—was, so Seymour always maintained, one of the greatest teachers imaginable. She could be, and frequently was, difficult, her corrections could be made without the slightest attempt to temper the wind to the shorn lamb, but she was complete mistress of her art, and given a willing and promising pupil was ready to take infinite pains to give generous instruction.

When the Kendals were planning a third tour of the States, Hicks felt that he owed it to himself to make a change. He would have played exactly the same parts had he joined the tour, boys, old men, character men, and he longed to play new parts. He always remembered with a certain satisfaction that the Kendals had to engage three actors to play the variety of parts which had been his, and which he had contrived to play during the tour.

He came to London, played for a short time with the great Mrs. John Wood, and then with J. L. Toole in Sir James Barrie's first play—*Walker London*. Seymour joined Toole's company when the great comedian was growing old, and his comedy was becoming slightly mechanical, but in his book, *Seymour Hicks*, he refers to Toole's wonderful eyes, and recalls that many great comedians have been noted for the beauty and expressive quality of their eyes. He quotes, J. L. Toole, Arthur Roberts, John Hare and "wonderful Fred Leslie". I would venture to add another—as Sir Henry Irving used to call him, the "Inimitable Mr. Leno". Marie Lloyd once said to me, "We laugh at Dan because if we didn't laugh we'd cry our eyes out. His are the saddest in the world." I have heard the same thing said of the great clown and comedian—Grimaldi.

After the successful run of *Walker London*, Seymour went to play in a new piece at the Court, called *The Other Fellow*. The run of *The Guardsman* at the Court was coming to an end, and one evening Seymour sat in the stalls taking "a busman's holiday" to watch the play. Ellaline Terriss made her entrance, Seymour recognized her as the girl he had seen in a manager's office five years previously. He realized that his memory of her as the most enchanting woman he had ever seen had not played him false. The very sight of her enslaved him! He went round and begged Arthur Chudleigh to introduce him!

"You'll meet her to-morrow on the stage," Chudleigh told him. "She is in the cast of the new play."

He was duly introduced the next morning, on the stage of the Court Theatre. Three weeks later they were married at Brentford. Ellaline had cabled to her father, then in America with Henry Irving's company, "Dear father, may I be engaged to Seymour Hicks. Love. Ella," to which William Terriss replied by cable, "Stop this nonsense. Wait for my return. Father."

However Ellaline's mother doubtless touched by the romantic aspect of two young, brilliant, and very-deeply-in-love young people, ranged herself firmly on their side.

"And so they were married and lived happily ever after." Seymour was twenty-two and Ellaline not yet twenty-one. The bridegroom's capital was twenty pounds. Young, clever, sharing the same profession and happy in their work, desperately in love, no wonder that their wedding breakfast at the Monico in Piccadilly Circus, which they reached by bus and train from Brentford, seemed to them both to be a Feast fit for the gods on high Olympus. It consisted of Irish stew and a bottle of Burgundy.

I have paid my small tribute to Ellaline Terriss in a book called *Me—and the Swans*, I am proud and happy to be counted among her friends. I am a fairly observant person and during the making of a film—*Glamour*—which Seymour Hicks both produced and played in, with Ellaline Terriss also appearing,

I was able to watch them both. I came to the conclusion that when young Seymour Hicks fell in love with her on the stage at the Court Theatre, or perhaps even five years earlier when he saw her for a moment in the drab office of a theatre manager, he did so with such complete thoroughness and so deeply that he remained in that blissful state for the remainder of his life.

I have written of how Seymour Hicks began his career, the rest of that career is shared with his wife. When recently I read a life of Lady Churchill, I thought how in many ways her treatment of Sir Winston resembled Ellaline's treatment of Seymour. Both men were unique characters, and consequently —difficult. Both had brains which were quick and brilliant, beyond those of ordinary mortals, both needed wives who loved them sufficiently well to understand them and to realize exactly how to deal with their characters and temperaments.

Seymour Hicks knew what almost incredible success meant, he built two theatres; he had to face patches of bad luck, when many men would have lost heart and become dispirited. For him there was always—"to-morrow is a lovely day!"

I have heard people—actors and actresses—declare that he was "impossible" both at rehearsals and also during the play itself. He loved "pace", and became intolerant and irritable with those people who did not achieve it. His own brain worked so rapidly that it seemed to me that he was always "a jump ahead", and unbearably irked by actors who lagged behind. Personally I met one producer who was exactly the same. Robert Courtneidge, father of Cicely Courtneidge. I have heard women say after a rehearsal, "What a brute that man is!", and have heard men describe him even more emphatically!

Then I realized, in part at least, the reason for these displays of temper, bursts of acute irritation, that regrettable vituperation, and all coming from two men who were fundamentally the kindest people imaginable, the most loyal of friends, and both possessing intelligence, to say nothing of their knowledge of stage-craft, far beyond the average. They were both highly

86

strung, and they both possessed great reputations in their profession. More, in most cases they were risking a great deal of money for which they had worked and worked very hard. Apart from their earnest wish to give the public an artistic, well-knitted show, a show which ran smoothly and was sufficiently polished. They risked reputation as producers and in Hicks' case as an actor in addition to the financial loss which an unpopular production caused them. So imagine Hicks producing a play, growing temperamental, allowing himself to rave, and be generally almost unreasonable, and think of how possible adverse notices would affect him.

"Rotten show, that new thing Hicks has put on! Badly produced! Very poor cast! He works his eye-brows off! Trying to pull the show together I suppose. No, it's a poor show."

Remember that the "star" is the person who draws in the public, that is why the stars have their name in lights over the entrance to the theatre. Jane Cakebread may draw her friends, possibly ten, twenty, thirty of them, she may develop into a very fine actress in the future—but it is *this particular production that counts.*

She is young, inexperienced, and she has had the inestimable privilege of having received instruction from a specialist in acting, and of being paid to be taught her job!

I've hated being slanged by a producer as much as anyone, but I long ago realized that the producer, particularly if he was an actor as well as the producer, carries the weight, and a very heavy weight it is too!

I remember a young actress who was playing with Hicks in *Vintage Wine*, in which I think I am right in saying, the wonderful Julia Neilson made her last appearance before she retired, saying to me, "He's a fiend at rehearsal. It's so unfair, he'd not speak to Julia Neilson as he speaks to me!"

"He doesn't need to," I said and left it at that. His own work was essentially vital, charged with vitality. He moved and spoke rapidly, but his enunciation was perfectly clear and he never moved without a reason. He told me that Mrs. Kendal instilled that precept into him. "Never move unless you know why you move." He brought gaiety on to the stage, he made you feel that he was enjoying the part he played and wanted you to share that enjoyment. Primarily I suppose that he was a comedian, a light comedian, but I have rarely seen an actor who could play a love scene more beautifully and with more perfect restraint. Pathos he could play without the faintest touch of banality.

I remember in *Mr. What's His Name* when he played the part of a man who has lost his memory, and becomes a successful hair-dresser. He is sent for to dress his wife's hair, and when he sees her his memory comes flooding back and he realizes that he is as much in love with her as ever. He discovers that she, thinking him dead, has married again and is completely happy. She does not recognize her original husband, and he does not disclose his identity. He sees her lawyer and—I think her brother, but I am quoting from memory and it is many, many years since I saw the play—they both tell him that for the sake of the wife he loves, to save a scandal, and to allow her life to go on tranquilly and undisturbed, he must—"forget to remember" and fade out of her life for the second time.

I can see the scene vividly still, and Seymour Hicks standing quite still, listening with an intensity that was almost painful to watch. I remember he looked pathetically lonely and very young as he listened, although at that time he must have been fifty-seven.

His adviser asked him if he understood, if he would do what they told him, pursue the course which they had mapped out? He nodded, then said, very simply, quietly, and with a pathos which was far more effective than wild protestations of his love for the woman would have been, "You see, I'm so fond of her." That was all.

I remember the man who was with me said as the curtain fell, "That was great acting."

I merely nodded, I couldn't have spoken had my life depended on it.

Again in *Sleeping Partners*, and here I know the lines always got a huge laugh, I personally found it desperately pathetic—as Seymour Hicks said it. The girl he loves—wildly, completely, and possibly not with that innate purity which was so admired by audiences until a few years ago, when they swung to the other extreme—had come to see him in his apartment. The play was, I think I am right, set in Paris. She complained of a headache, and he rushed away to bring her a draught which was an infallible cure. Gratefully and charmingly she thanked him. I saw the play when Ellaline Terriss played the part, so it follows automatically that her gratitude was expressed charmingly, and almost immediately fell asleep. Distractedly the devoted lover realizes that he has given her a sleeping draught by mistake! It is guaranteed to keep her asleep for hours and hours. In despair he kneels beside the couch where she lies sleeping tranquilly, and says, "I wanted to be your lover— and I'm only your night-watchman."

It was the curtain line for that act, the audience roared with laughter, to me the line was always completely pathetic. I never liked his "Scrooge", I never liked Bransby Williams' Scrooge either, I never liked anyone as Scrooge, and when I played it for the troops one Christmas during the last war, I hated myself whole-heartedly. It is what is so fittingly—if crudely—called "a tear-jerker", plus the fact that it is "ham" and not even good ham at that, and if it is to have any impact on an audience it must be painted in broad, violent colours, splashed on heavily and without the faintest trace of shade or skilful gradations of colour. Emphatically Scrooge was not a particularly suitable character for Seymour Hicks. His audiences loved it. A woman once said to me, "You'd never think that it was Seymour Hicks, would you?" That was one of the faults I found with Scrooge.

His career is known to everyone, everyone at least who has been a theatre-goer all their lives, or people who revel in theatre records and theatre history. He went from success to success, true he faced disaster, and emerged possibly "bloody" but certainly "unbowed", or if he did bear traces of what he had been through during one of these financial crises, he hid them carefully from his public.

His wit remained as spontaneous as ever, his heart never ceased to be kind and filled with a willingness to be friendly. He was one of the most appreciative and generous men I have ever met. I had the honour of playing in a film in which he played and also produced, or does one say "directed" when speaking of films? He played an elderly actor, still fascinating, still desperately attractive. A young girl—Margot Graham played the part, I remember, and beautiful she looked too—fell in love with him, and he with her. Realizing that he is too old for her, that she should marry the young and estimable young man who dogged her footsteps and was eminently suitable, the actor sets himself to disillusion her. It's an old story—it was done in a score of plays, the method by which the disillusionment was achieved was simply to get, or pretend to get, exceedingly drunk. In one scene the girl visits the actor in his dressing-room, and Seymour told me that he proposed for one brief moment to allow his emotion to master him and to take the girl in his arms, thus registering for a few feet of film the real state of his feeling for her. What did I think of the idea?

I said, "She's alone in your dressing-room! The 'nice people' in the audience will say, 'He's behaving like a damned cad!', the ordinary human people will be disappointed when after that very brief display of passion, you open the door and say 'Good night'. Don't touch her!"

He stared at me, then said, "My God, you're right!"

Later he told everyone, you might have imagined that I had suggested some remarkable piece of brilliance which would make the film worthy of an Oscar!

I could give a dozen instances of the exaggerated gratitude Hicks felt and expressed towards anyone who did him the smallest service, or made the least suggestion regarding a play which he felt to have value.

He loved giving presents to people, he gave me what was known as "The Keane Star"—a beautiful order used by Henry Irving when he played Louis XI. In the centre is a lovely piece of dark, rich blue enamel, with the letter "L" inset in the enamel. Hicks bought it at the Irving sale, and gave it to me. After several years I felt that the star "belonged" to the theatre, and sent it by Angela du Maurier, who was paying me a visit here in Italy, to give to that beloved man, Ivor Novello. He was playing in his last musical play at the time, and wore it every night in that touching last act of *King's Rhapsody*. I still have his letter expressing his pleasure in possessing such a thing, something which had belonged to "three great men of the theatre—Keane, Irving and Seymour Hicks". When Ivor left us, Bobby Andrews asked me if the star might go to Laurence Olivier.

I dare not begin to tell examples of Seymour's wit and his unfailing sense of humour, first because he has told many of them in his own books—his life, *Chestnuts Re-roasted*, and others, and secondly because I should find myself crowding out everyone else in this book. Sufficient to say that when you hear a particularly clever piece of repartee, or an especially good story told with the preface, "I remember once—" or "An amusing thing happened to me—", you can safely murmur, "Ten to one it's something Seymour Hicks said or did."

When the honour of knighthood was conferred upon him, I stopped to speak to a woman who used to sell matches outside the Ivy, I said, "You've seen that Seymour Hicks is now Sir Seymour?" She smiled broadly," I saw it, ducks! They may have made 'im Sir Semer, an' 'er Lady 'Icks, they'll alwais be dear Semer 'Icks an' darlin' little Ellaline Terriss to us."

That reflects how their public felt and still feels about them.

VIII

GEORGE WOOD, O.B.E.
(Wee Georgie Wood)

I HAVE known him for more years than I care to count, I
have always admired him both as an artist and a man,
and except during those brief intervals when we have
been passing through the aftermath of one of our fairly numerous
differences of opinion, I have always felt for him the same great
affection which I believe he has for me.

These differences of opinion have invariably been over
something completely trivial; on the other hand when either
of us has pursued a course of which the other has disapproved
and which actually was something fairly grave or important,
neither of us has said a word!

Our first meeting was in Middlesbrough where George was
playing in pantomime, with beautiful Marguerite Broadfoote
playing the Prince, and Ernest Reeves—poor brave fellow
that he was—playing the dame. I forget how or where we
met, but my memory is of a small attractive boy of about
twelve, with twinkling eyes and a nice wide smile, wearing a
particularly good tweed over-coat and a cap to match. He
denies that he ever had such a coat, but I am firm on the point,
because I remember his confiding to me that the pockets were
lined with velvet.

I saw his act in pantomime, and hardened as I was, even so
many years ago, to see fine artists, that scene of Georgie
Wood's impressed me tremendously. That was before that
grand woman Dolly Harmer played with him. His partner,
she played his nurse in those early days, was Ethel Cosgrove of

the double turn Cosgrove and Burns. She was very good, but she never reached the heights of fine acting that were achieved later by Dolly Harmer. Admittedly Dolly had greater scope, because in a few years George discarded the "child act", and played small, impertinent but distinctly lovable small boys. Dolly then became his stage "mother", and a fine performance she always gave too. For years she travelled with him, visiting America, Africa and Australia. When the Second World War began she went with him working for E.N.S.A. to entertain the troops overseas. Nothing came amiss to Dolly Harmer, radio, the discomforts which went hand in hand with transport during their E.N.S.A. tours of Africa, Egypt and the Middle East. She took them all in her stride as only good troupers can—and do. She cared nothing for heat or cold, for long uncomfortable journeys, only two things really mattered to Dolly—Georgie and the show.

She and Bella Marshall—who for many years acted as George's dresser and is now his admirable housekeeper—both conspired to the best of their ability, to stand between George and whatever was cold, unfriendly or inimical.

When Dolly died, her loss was the greatest ever sustained by this strange, complicated, often puzzled, over-sensitive man known as George Wood.

I remember talking to George when he contemplated going to Australia for a very long stay, he had tempting offers to produce plays, a thing he has always found very attractive, he had a long list of lecture dates and the prospect of a future which appeared to be brilliant. He told me that he might stay two years, possibly more, possibly decide to remain out there. He had asked Dolly to go with him.

"What does she feel about it?" I asked.

George shrugged his shoulders. "Undecided," he said. "She can't quite make up her mind. I'm worried——"

I said, "Will you tell her that if she doesn't want to go, because after all it does mean uprooting herself, I'll go. I could play 'Mrs Robinson', not as well as Dolly plays her, I admit, but I'm not a bad actress. Give Dolly my love and tell her that I'll take good care of you."

George delivered my message of course, and equally "of course", I never went to Australia, and Dolly did. It was an old trick, but it had worked as I felt certain that it would.

I have wandered away from George himself, but Dolly's devotion to him is a valuable sidelight on his character as well as hers. The late Miriam Warner had the same deep affection for him, though possibly in a slightly different way and in a lesser degree. I have met Miriam and asked casually, "Have you seen George?"

"No, I have not, and I have no particular wish to, either."

"What's wrong?"

"He's—impossible!"

I loved and admired Miriam, I knew her very well, and our friendship was based on a very sound foundation, but she, herself, was not incapable of being—impossible!

The next time I saw her, she would say in the course of conversation, "When I was having dinner with George last Tuesday——" or "George took me to see Yvonne Arnaud in *Dear Charles* last week." George told her this or that.

"So everything is smooth sailing again?" I'd ask.

"Of course. I can't go on nursing grievances with George!"

However, to return to George himself.

He was born in Jarrow. The year does not matter, only I am sure that it is far later than most people believe. On the stage or in variety, probably in any form of entertainment business, people are invariably credited with far more years than they actually possess.

The year Marie Lloyd died, I heard people state with conviction that she was "nearly seventy"—she was barely in her middle fifties. Only this year, I was assured that Sophie Tucker might possibly give her age as seventy-six, but that actually she was "well over eighty". A week after I had been on television with Evelyn Laye, sitting opposite to her under lights which were cruelly bright and concentrated, to watch her

looking completely ravishing and far less than what her actual
age must inevitably be, I was told that she was "nearer seventy
than sixty". Dorothy Ward who my reason and my memory
tell me must be over sixty, and looks about forty-five, is credited
with anything from eighty-five to ninety.

I don't know George Wood's age, I could easily find out but
it doesn't interest me. I only know that it is a long time since
I first met him, and obviously he must be older than he was
then. I leave it at that.

His parents were normally sized people, I never actually
knew either of them. I once asked George what his mother
was like and he replied, "Like me in a bonnet."

He was a bright child, with a remarkable and retentive
memory. Like most children he loved "dressing up", and also
in common with the majority of children enjoyed appearing
before an audience in some capacity or other.

He was at a very early age in great demand for concerts,
"anniversaries", benefits and the like. I gather that the
guineas and half guineas which he earned were not unaccept-
able as an addition to the family exchequer. I believe that at
this time his mother was going through a difficult time and
facing certain matrimonial difficulties. Facing them with
indomitable courage and determination.

She was intensely proud of her small son, and prided herself
on always "keeping him nice", an expression demonstrating
itself in those days by dressing the unfortunate child in dreadful
clothes somewhat after the style of Lord Fauntleroy. Later
when he came to be known by the public of the Tyneside, he
was dressed in Eton suits. There is a photograph of him wearing one, and looking almost choked by the wide, white collar.

He began his professional career with a company of Cosgrove and Burns. The story continues of how he went from
strength to strength, until in Bradford he was seen by Ernest
Edelsten, the variety agent. Edelsten's wife was the beautiful
Marguerite Broadfoote, and she always maintained that she
first saw Georgie appearing at a Police Concert at which she

was singing. He was then doing his "child act" and a charming act it was. He appeared as a child who is still dreaming of the pantomime to which it has been taken by its relatives. Left alone in his night nursery, the child imitates the various artists who appeared in the pantomime. There was a certain amount of "patter" with his nurse, but the weight of the turn was carried by—Wee Georgie Wood. Marguerite was impressed by this little boy—he was only about nine at the time—and mentioned him to her husband. Ernest Edelsten, one of the best known variety agents at the time, saw the act and—became George's agent.

He became more than his agent, I believe that George was one of the few people for whom Edelsten had a genuine affection. He was a curious man, very good looking and with a certain charm when he chose to exercise it. His education was, I imagine, exceedingly limited. In business he was brilliant and relentless. He boasted that he could "make stars", and he undoubtedly was capable of furthering their interests—and his own—to almost incredible lengths. Whatever obstacle stood in his way—whether that obstacle were human or circumstantial—must either remove itself, or Ernest Edelsten walked over it.

In George here was the makings of a star, he recognized that this diminutive child possessed a particularly active brain in addition to natural talent. I always think that it flattered his vanity that George, then impressionable and maleable—to a certain extent—either instinctively or by design, modelled himself on Edelsten. Already he was building one of those facades from behind which George Wood hid from the world around him.

He copied Edelsten's form of speech, using short, rather abrupt sentences, and cultivating a slightly over-done dignity, which he admits was to conceal his natural inferiority complex caused by his size. Happily for George and those around him, the imitation did not last very long. George had never had the benefit or limitations, whichever way you look at it, of an extensive and expensive education; he possessed a mentality which was hungry for education, and he—gave that education to himself.

He read omnivorously, and has continued to do so. I find it difficult to make a reference to some quotation in classical literature, to some particular school of thought, to some newly evolved theory involving humanity, to refer to some play which has impressed me—and how regrettably few they are in these days—without discovering that George knows far more about all of these things than I do.

So George discarded his imitation of Ernest Edelsten and although I sometimes detect faint echoes of that great variety agent's testy manner, the rest has disappeared. I was only fortunate enough to see Sir Henry Irving twice in my life, I was very young and he was growing very old, but I remember his voice clearly. I have been faintly reminded of Irving's delivery of words when George has been speaking of some matter in which he is deeply interested.

At the time, shortly after he met Edelsten, George was well on his way to stardom, in a very few years he attained and securely held that position, never to lose it until he finally retired from active service on the Variety Stage.

He was top of the bill everywhere he went. His salary bounded upwards, and he was sought after by managers in America, Africa and Australia. Dolly Harmer had by the time George reached the zenith of his popularity, taken the place of Ethel Burns as his stage mother. His one-act sketches, "Mrs. Robinson and her son, Georgie" were unique. They contained all the necessary ingredients which made an appeal to the public. They were "homely", they were that thing beloved by the public—domestic comedy. That particular brand of play, whether of three acts or merely sketch length, which has invariably been a success, provided that it is played with sincerity and written by someone who knows how the innately, highly well-conducted lower middle class really speak and live. "Mrs. Robinson" was obviously a woman who "kept herself to herself" and Dolly Harmer made her as real as Elsie and Doris Waters have made their "Gert and Daisy". George was a typical intelligent, impudent, warm-hearted boy, indulged by his mother to a certain extent, but conscious that with her he could go so far and no further.

There was often a streak of pathos in those sketches, which at times made me uncomfortable because they did tend occasionally to develop into—not very good—ham! However the public liked it, and elderly women would remove a tear with the corner of a handkerchief, sniff a little and give it as their opinion that, "He's a good lad, yes, for all his cheek and imperince, 'is 'eart's in the right place."

George while still with comparatively few years behind him was a success, a bill topper, an idol of the public.

He was not only accepted but welcomed by his fellow artistes, he joined the Water Rats, the great Variety society, which like the Lady Ratlings does so much towards helping deserving charities and assisting fellow artistes who have fallen on bad times. He held various offices in the Society and was finally chosen as King Rat for the year, an office held by many of the greatest names in Variety.

He appeared on the radio, or rather he spoke on the radio and appeared on television. He was made an honorary member of numerous clubs, among them the Ancient Order of Buffaloes. This election was held somewhere on Tyne-side, and the following morning George was walking in the town with one of the Members of the Lodge to which he had been admitted. They met a friend of this member of the lodge, an ancient gentleman, one of the City Fathers, who was proud of his ability to "speak his mind" without fear or favour.

The Member of the Buffaloes greeted him, and said, "This is Georgie Wood. We made him a Buffalo last night."

The City Father looked George over appraisingly, and said, "Naay, there's not enough o' that one to mak' a Nannie-goat let alone a Buffalo!"

He was admittedly one of the best after-dinner speakers in

London, and was in great request. He never minded accepting the aid of the toast-master to help him to stand on a chair to deliver his speech, and did so without the slightest sign of embarrassment, in consequence causing none to his listeners.

He had developed great composure and dignity. He also cultivated the gift of suiting his conversation to his company. In other words he "never put a foot wrong".

I wish that I could convey adequately the development of this man, for in it I find much to admire. Life for a man of considerable mental attainment, who is born to be much less in stature than his fellow men, almost inevitably once he is of an age to realize the limits which have been placed on his activities by his lack of inches, develops an inferiority complex. Either he becomes hypersensitive, hating to be seen and stared at except —if he is on the stage—by the audience, or he cultivates a bombastic, over-bearing attitude towards people, seeking on every possible occasion to assert himself, and to demonstrate— to his own satisfaction at least, that he is their superior in everything except actual size.

I have known two men who were diminutives, and they both rose superior to their size. One was Harry Relph, known in Variety and to the public as Little Tich, and the other is Georgie Wood. Both of these men were fortunate in having intellects above the ordinary quality, and both cultivated them assiduously, building with them a facade to hide their inborn sense of inferiority. Not only were these facades built for the benefit of the world at large, but also to "boost" themselves to themselves.

Harry Relph used to read until night had turned to day, he studied the cello and became an excellent cellist. W. H. Squire, the famous cellist, and a great friend of Harry Relph's once said, "Thank Heaven that Harry stuck to variety and didn't become a professional musician! I know of at least one cellist— myself—who would have been seriously disturbed had he done so!" Harry Relph studied painting, and while his work was always obviously that of an amateur, it was the work of a "gifted amateur". He spoke French perfectly, was decorated and awarded the Legion of Honour for his contribution to the world of entertainment and wore the ribbon in his button-hole with considerable pride.

His facade was complete!

He cared very little for meeting extraneous people, he preferred a few chosen friends, and shunned those gatherings of Variety and Theatrical people, which are invariably full of good humour, warmth and spontaneous friendliness. With his intimate friends he could be charming, amusing and often very witty.

He earned tremendous salaries, and once someone in conversation with him said, "I'm told that you earn more every year than a Prime Minister." Harry Relph answered with one of his charming smiles, which could be completely cold and was reserved for people who made such statements, "I believe so, but then I do so much less harm."

George Wood has made just such another facade—and again not only to hide him from the world, but to hide him from himself. In other words after the first novelty of being a "bill topper", of earning a very large salary, and seeing himself constantly referred to in the press, wore off a little, he realized that he hated being a variety artist, disliked the life which the music halls offered, and began to take George Wood in hand and "remake him nearer to the heart's desire".

He was far too good an artist, had far too much North Country sound commonsense not to continue to do his work to the very best of his ability. There have been times when his acute perception has told him that he has given a poor show, that he was not working at the top of his form and he has been deeply ashamed and angry—of and with himself.

He liked to meet intellectuals, and realized that in order to do so he must equip himself mentally in order to make himself acceptable to them. Like Harry Relph, he set to work to educate himself. Like the majority of stage children, travelling as they do from town to town each week, his education had been spasmodic and intermittent. He set to work to fill in the gaps. I have an idea that he reads "who-dunnits" as light relief from the heavier books into which he plunges. On matters concerning the theatre and variety legal contracts, matters political—not only British politics but international affairs, his knowledge is profound. He is a great play-goer and his criticisms are well defined, and invariably trenchant.

His Eminence Cardinal Griffin was a great friend of George's, they had been friends when the "Little Cardinal" was an ordinary priest, deeply interested in some local orphanage. George appeared for him at some charity concert, and so their friendship began.

When *The Song of Bernadette* was released, the Cardinal went to the first showing, and the press came clamouring to the Archbishop's House at Westminster to know what his reactions had been. It happened that George was sitting talking to the Cardinal when his secretary entered to say that the Press were asking for His Eminence's opinion of the film.

Cardinal Griffin said, "I enjoyed it," then with that lovable almost boyish wide smile of his, he added, "I admit that parts of it amused me considerably——"

George almost shot out of his chair, "No, no!" he said almost excitedly. "That won't do at all! Can't you see the head-line—Cardinal finds *The Song of Bernadette* amusing! Cardinal laughs at *The Song of Bernadette*! No, no!" then he subsided, slightly confused because he had forgotten that he was speaking to the Head of the Catholic Church in England.

This time the Cardinal did laugh!

"You're right, George," he said, "quite right." Then turning to his secretary he added with humorous gravity, "Whenever we are asked for an opinion of any matter connected with the stage or screen, telephone to Mr. Wood and get his advice."

There is a strong strain of what you might term—reasoned humility in George. He was going to Rome, and through the good offices of some of his important Catholic friends, the promise of a private audience with Pope John was given to him. He arrived in Rome, his audience was arranged for the following morning. On the journey he had been thinking, thinking hard. His Holiness was probably as busy as any man in the world, he had to concentrate on problems which were vitally affecting the Church and the administration of its affairs mundane and spiritual. Moreover the Pope was an old man, he might almost boast of his "toughness", and strength, but —he was an old man.

Why, George asked himself, should I be given time so that he may speak to me? I'm robbing him, and through him the Church of time which is very precious. It's not fair and I won't do it!

He went to the Vatican, obtained an interview with the Cardinal in charge of the arrangements for audiences, both public and private. Respectfully, and modestly George stated his case, adding that with all due respect, might he be allowed to ask that his audience could be cancelled?

Very calmly, probably formally—for urbanity is not a necessary quality in Cardinals—George was told to leave his address in Rome, and that the matter would receive attention.

Comparatively late that evening a letter was delivered to him, by hand, from the Vatican. He was to present himself at the Vatican the following morning and the hour was stated.

The next morning he saw the same Cardinal.

"His Holiness wishes to see you, Mr. Wood, as arranged." Suddenly, his eyes twinkled. He did not even then look urbane, he looked very human.

"Your visit to me yesterday was duly reported to the Holy Father. He insisted on the arrangement for an audience being adhered to, and—shall I tell you why? Because of the reasons which you gave as prompting you to be asked to be excused from not presenting yourself. Had you not given those reasons, it is possible that the Holy Father might have cancelled or postponed the audience. He is very busy indeed. Now, I shall take you to the audience, Mr. Wood."

So George was ushered into the presence of that Pope who was probably one of the best loved men in the world. He spoke through an interpreter, for unlike Pope Pius he had no English. He was kind, very human, George told me, his eyes twinkled with good humour, and yet you felt the innate wisdom and goodness of the man.

Among other things he said, through the interpreter of course, but as he spoke George heard the chuckle, "They've made me Pope, but I'm still—a parish priest!"

There were times when the facade which George had built so carefully showed cracks and fissures, I never saw him cast himself for the rôle of "Broken Hearted Clown", but there were times when I knew that he was terribly unhappy. His marriage was not a success. I never knew or saw his wife, but he assured me that she was very charming, and very attractive. An American vaudeville artist. The marriage was dissolved. For a time I thought that he might throw in his lot completely with the Oxford Group; we never discussed their aims, or their faith. George knew, I think, my feelings about it all, and it was not my business to either discuss them with him—for or against.

In one letter written at a time when I think George felt that the world was a rather cold, inimical sort of place, he wrote at the end of a letter which reflected his depression, "I know that I shall feel better when I am a Catholic."

I made no comment when I replied, and not until a considerable time had elapsed did he write to say that he had been received and was very happy. Later he sent me a book of prayers, and in it he wrote: "To Mickie, who had so much to do with making this real to me. Love from George."

We never discuss religion, we talk of the stage, of variety, of politics, and the books we have read. I feel that a great deal of the facade has been demolished because it is no longer a necessity. He is another "self-made man", and as we say in the North, "He's made a pretty good job of it."

Don't imagine that in joining the Catholic Church George has turned himself into a plaster saint. Nothing could be further from the truth. It happened that he discovered that he needed, as most of us do if we admit it, something which was essentially stable. Something which had rules, stated beliefs from which it will not and cannot deviate. The Catholic Church exercises discipline over its members, and discipline is something which is beneficial to a large percentage of humanity. In other words the Catholic Church provided a spiritual diet which suited George—as I found that it suited me. There are people, millions of them to whom as a diet it is not only unpalatable but completely indigestible.

He remains after all these years my very good friend, I admired him as an artist, for having stuck to work which he did not really like and having given to that work the best he had. He has cultivated his brain, given it plenty of work to do, and in consequence it has remained active and alert. His sense of humour is very good, unless he happens to be in one of his "testy" moods, then I consider him—as he considers me— tiresome and unreasonable.

He surmounted the handicap which nature imposed upon him, even turned it into an asset. His praise of his friends is generous, not particularly to them, but to people who refer to them. He may say to me, as a kind of afterthought, "I liked your last book," that is all. To others he is more expansive and generous in his approval of my work. My name cropped up somewhere, and George said, "Ah, yes, the peripatetic novelist." The man to whom he spoke said to me later, "Funny fellow, Georgie, said that you were peripatetic. Was he being complimentary or plain rude. What the deuce does it mean?"

One last word. It happened on Easter Day, George was chained to the house through an injury to his knee. He sat watching High Mass relayed from Saint Peter's, Rome, because he was unable to go to the Cathedral.

His wonderful housekeeper, Bella (Miss Marshall) opened the door and glanced at the television screen. "Ugh!" she ejaculated with restrained scorn, "George Black did that fifteen years ago!"

There is my impression of George Wood, O.B.E. I realize that I have not mentioned his decoration. I have a very vague idea as to why it was bestowed, and if that idea is correct—and I believe that it is—he fully deserved it. I asked him why it had been given to him, he pursed his lips and thought hard, then shook his head, "I can't tell you. If people ask you, you can tell them that it was—not—for entertaining the troops for E.N.S.A!"

So I stick to my own—vague—idea.

IX

SIR GEORGE ROBEY
Prime Minister of Mirth

EOPLE used to say that he had been "to Oxford", very probably he had and so have many of us, but I never heard him state that he had been a member of any college, or actually studied at the University. What actually happened was that he was intended to be a student at the University, and then his father's investments dropped, failed or somehow vanished into thin air and that was the end of the dream of a university career for George Robey.

Instead he went to Birmingham to study engineering. He hated it, mechanics, machinery, bolts, screws and the rest of it made not the slightest appeal to him, what he remembered most clearly was that the men were always drinking—cups of tea.

He was in the office of the works and he liked office work even less than he liked the machinery. George longed for London and home. He had made friends in Birmingham and won some local fame as a mandolinist, which he played with another young man who played the guitar. Together they appeared at charity concerts, benefits, and other excellent halls where efforts were being made to raise money for some equally excellent cause. The artists gave their services and all that young George and his friend collected were the profuse thanks of the organisers.

So George returned to London, and lived in his parents' house on Brixton Hill. He was still working as a budding engineer, and liking it no better as months passed. He knew practically nothing about the music hall, his chief interest was the theatre. One evening some friends asked him to go with them to the Westminster Aquarium. They wanted to see the great—all magicians, mesmerists and conjurers were billed as "Great" in those days—Professor Kennedy, the mesmerist. One of George's friends knew Kennedy and promised an introduction to him after the performance.

They watched the show, saw the group of people who had "offered" themselves as subjects for Professor Kennedy's wonderful powers. They saw them do strange things, eat candles with apparent gusto, drink cold water out of a huge glass and testify that it was whisky and to prove that it was, staggered about the stage in apparent intoxication. Later they went round and met the Professor. He was a kindly, jovial fellow, and George told him that he wouldn't mind sitting on the stage during his act, and—apparently—allow himself to be mesmerized. The professor hesitated, then asked, "Why?" George replied, "Then when I'm mesmerized, you can tell me that I'm a comic singer, and that I'm to sing a song."

The young man with the fresh coloured face, the remarkable eyebrows and the intelligent, bright eyes, impressed the Professor.

"All right. Start to-morrow if you like."

"Only," young Robey insisted, "no sticking needles into me, no eating coke or pepper! Just—a comic song."

The following evening the Professor moved among the audience and came to a halt in front of George. He made a few passes before the boy's face, the boy seemed confused for a moment, then his eyes became blank, and he rose from his stall. Kennedy said in a deep impressive voice, "Follow me!"

Walking as if he were a sleep-walker, George followed him on to the stage where several other victims were already seated. More passes before George's blank, expressionless face, then again Kennedy's ringing voice. "You are in my power! You are a comic singer. There is a piano over there. Go and stand near it, and sing your song. Rise!"

George rose, walked steadily to the O.P. side of the stage, and began to sing *A little peach in an orchard grew*, a song which was very popular at the time. The audience loved it, and George decided to try a second verse. He had been given a careful wink of approval from the Professor, but one of the other victims resented the fact that George was "stealing the show" and, rushing down the stage, planted a hearty kick, which had the effect of sending George flying into the stalls, where he landed on top of an old and dignified gentleman. To the accompaniment of roars of laughter from the audience George disentangled himself, and sat down in an empty seat next to the still protesting old gentleman. He stared round him, as if bewildered—as he no doubt was—and saw Kennedy standing on the stage watching him with a fixed and meaningful stare. George picked up his cue—when did he ever miss one?—and rising, standing on the seat, he continued the second verse of his song from the exact point where the kick had interrupted him.

The audience were delighted and roared their approval; the song ended and Kennedy descending from the stage took George back to it, and pushed him into a chair. He then proceeded to "release him from mesmeric power" with a few mysterious passes.

Professor Kennedy was delighted, and invited George to come as often as he liked and become a "victim", George enjoyed doing so, and enjoyed singing his comic songs to an appreciative audience. Kennedy never gave him any salary, but when the manager of the Oxford Music came, heard George and asked him, "How would you like to try your luck at Saturday matinée at the Oxford?" and George thrilled and delighted jumped at the chance, Kennedy gave him a diamond which George had set as a tie-pin. His first piece of jewellery.

The Saturday matinées at the Oxford were well known, each week the management would give a "trial show" to some unknown artiste, and if they were acceptable to the audience, offered them an engagement.

George, full of excitement, not unmixed with trepidation,

duly appeared. After his turn the manager came to him and asked him if he would care to go on again for the evening performance. He warned the young man, "They're a critical lot, not easily pleased. Still if you like to—have a go——"

George emphatically—did like! On the same programme were some of the greatest names in Variety, and among them "The Sisters Lloyd". This act was composed of, in all probability, Marie Lloyd's sister Rosie, and Bella Burge, later to become the wife of Dick Burge, at one time the champion prize-fighter in England.

George went on, and the audience showed their delight. The result was the Manager came round to see him, and offered him a twelve months' contract to appear at the Oxford. George went home, walking most of the way because his heart and his feet felt so light that it was no effort to cover the long distance to Brixton.

Several times, so he used to say, he looked up at the stars shining so placidly, and raised his hat, saying, "Good evening, gentlemen. I am one of you now—or I shall be one day."

While he worked out his once-nightly appearance at the Oxford, he was allowed to take other engagements provided they did not interfere with his appearance at the Oxford. He appeared at most of the halls in London, and came to be known and hailed by their audiences. Bow, the Foresters, the Bedford, the "Met." in Edgware Road, the Holborn, the Canterbury, the Empress Brixton, and many more—alas, now they have vanished. The old Metropolitan stood its ground longer than most of them, but that has now closed its door and is due for demolition. For all I know it may be demolished already as I write this.

Variety, that typically English form of entertainment has suffered what—I believe and that belief is shared by my good friend, Charlie Chester—is a temporary eclipse. We believe that Variety will rise again like the phoenix, possibly not in exactly the same form, but it will still be—Variety.

At the time when young George Robey began his career

Variety was just beginning its boom. Music Halls were being built, larger and more splendid buildings rising all over London and in the provinces. That pioneer of Variety, Edward Moss, later Sir Edward Moss, coined a very apt phrase regarding this form of entertainment, "Pot house to palace", for the music halls actually did begin in the taverns of England. The landlord engaged the players for a week, he wrote their names in soap on a big looking glass. In those days you were not "top of the bill" but "top of the glass". Sometimes he paid a weekly salary, sometimes the performer was allowed to go among the audience "bottling", that is collecting, after he had done his turn.

The form of entertainment grew in popularity, the audience sat at tables, and were served with liquid refreshment, and even such delicacies as pork pies, hot mutton pies, pigs' trotters and the like. Edward Moss in Edinburgh, being a young man of vision and with a touch of actual genius in his make-up, began the first real music hall as the British people came to know it. Charles Morton "raised" it, giving it an air of respectability, for the halls were regarded as places practically reserved for men in their early days. I can remember my headmistress, when I was a teacher, calling me to her desk, and asking in a voice filled with cold disapproval, if it were true that I visited the Empire every week? Then on July 1st, 1912, King George the Fifth ordered a Royal Command Performance at the Palace Theatre, London. Incidentally this is the only Variety "Royal Command Performance" ever given, and again, I think that it was Sir Edward Moss who coined the apt phrase, "The Cinderella of the Arts has gone to the ball at last."

George Robey began his brilliant career when the music halls were approaching their highest popularity. There were giants in those days and he quickly became one of them. Those were the days when the demand for "turns" exceeded the supply, and artists played several different halls a night. In his admirable book, *Looking Back on Life*, George tells how he worked the Metropolitan, drove on in his brougham—then the hall mark of the successful artist—to Collins in Islington—back to the Oxford, and on to the Pavilion. That was what popularity meant in those days, good money undoubtedly but the artists earned every penny of their salaries. True, there were a good many performers who only enjoyed a brief popularity and then—faded out. They were the people who were content to "rest on their laurels" or had not the intelligence to study the tastes and requirements of various audiences. George Robey being a man of great—I might almost say supreme—intelligence studied his audiences, and realized very quickly, for example, that his famous song, *Clarence, the Last of the Dandies* when sung to an audience, at the Forester's in Whitechapel, or the Bedford, Camden Town, needed to be delivered at a much quicker tempo than that which he used at the Oxford or the Tivoli. Harry Lauder realized the same thing. I have heard him at the Alhambra, Glasgow singing with the broadest possible Scottish accent, I have heard him again at the Palace, London, sing the same song in what his own country-men would have stigmatized as being "awfu' English-ified."

George too was a firm believer in "keeping fit", he loved games, and never lost an opportunity of playing cricket or tennis. "The real game of tennis," he would say, "is the finest game ever invented. Not—allow me to insist—lawn tennis, but the game as it was played on a court by kings of France and England four hundred years and more ago." As a sprinter in his younger days he was very successful having won races of considerable importance. He declared that after sixty a man should eat only one full meal a day, if he wanted to keep fit.

Had he not been the great actor that he undoubtedly was, he might have been a successful artist, I have seen some of his works and had he devoted himself entirely to that branch of art—for I hold the one which he chose to be among the Arts—there is little doubt that he would have been highly successful.

As a recreation he drew caricatures and drew them remarkably well too. I have several—one of himself, and another of the same man playing Sancho Panza in the film he made of *Don Quixote*. He made violins, surely one of the most difficult works to attempt by an amateur. Made them so well too, that the great Fritz Kreisler, who was one of his personal friends—accepted one which George had made, and actually played one of the items in his programme on it at the Albert Hall. George was no mean performer on the violin himself.

One evening Kreisler visited him in his dressing room, and while the dresser was absent on some errand, Kreisler examined a violin which George had just finished making. He picked up a bow, and began to play on it, marvelling at the excellent tone. George listened entranced. The piece of music finished, the great violinist laid down the violin, and congratulated George on his achievement.

Shortly after he bade George good-night and left. A moment later the dresser entered, and eyed the violin and his master with even more than usual respect. Presently he said, "May I just say, sir, that I heard your playing just now as I came along the passage. Lovely! There's no doubt you're improving, sir, in your violin playing." George did not correct him! He told the story to Kreisler later, and the great man was tremendously amused.

From the music halls, George entered the musical comedy stage. Those who remember him in *The Bing Boys are here*, and *The Bing Boys on Broadway* with that charming woman and fine artist Vi Loraine can recall what a success both of these productions were. Vi Loraine, Alfred Lester and George Robey made an unforgettable trio, and the wonderful song, *The only girl in the world* still is popular and still brings nostalgic memories. Then followed *Round in Fifty*, and *Bits and Pieces* which seemed as if it would run for ever. I remember too very clearly *Helen* with that lovely actress "Boo" (Evelyn) Laye playing Helen and George playing Menelaus a superb production, and most admirable characterization. Then came Sancho Panza in the film of *Don Quixote*, and Falstaff in *Henry IV*.

Nothing appeared to be beyond the powers of George Robey. I don't suggest that he could—or ever wanted to—play romantic parts, but anything which demanded comedy, and comedy of a very high order, seemed within his capacity. His versatility was amazing.

Many years ago, it must be at least bordering on fifty, I was at a matinée at the Palladium. George was on the bill, and I went round to see him. Very modestly, and kindly, he gave me a book which he had written. It was called *Pause*, and on the cover was the white gloved hand of a policeman in the act of holding up the traffic. I remember that the large white hand against the dark background was very telling. He wrote my name in it, at my request, and I bore the book away in triumph, mentally promising myself a pleasant time laughing over it. I thought that the title was possibly a play on the words "Pause" and "Paws". That night I began to read it, and to my surprise and, I admit, faint disappointment, I found it to be a profound book, unless memory plays me false—and after fifty years that is quite possible—it dealt with Eastern religions. Alas, I took it down to my dressing room the following night, and some-one—a visitor I presume—appropriated it, as George would have said, "In other words—pinched it!" I have never been able to get another copy, though I have sought for one in every second-hand book shop I could find.

He also wrote his own life, *Looking back on Life*, and frankly it is a great deal better than the majority of theatrical recollections. It is full of good stories, there is generous praise for his friends and the artists he admired; there is admirable restraint —and judicious praise—concerning the people—I remember them—whom he might admire as artists but never really liked personally.

He is not afraid to voice his opinions and voice them pretty loudly too. He loved melody, and refused to accept most of the syncopated and jazz "music" that was unloaded on British audiences. He was more than only knowledgeable concerning objets d'art, and I have seen his collection of china, porcelain, glass and crystal and it obviously reflects the taste of a man who knew "what was what". He was generous to a fault, his wife, who was Blanche Littler, told me once, "George never has any money in his pocket! Oh, he has some when he goes out, but he never comes home with any. He always finds someone to give it to!"

George Robey was married twice, the first time to that very attractive and clever artist, Ethel Haydon. She was a charming person, I knew her quite well, and always enjoyed meeting her. They had two children, a son and daughter. The son finished his education at Jesus College, Cambridge, studied for the Bar and became a most successful and popular character in legal circles. The daughter, Eileen, is an artist, so she has inherited her father's artistic gifts, as his son has inherited his high intelligence.

His second wife was Blanche Littler, the sister of Emile and Prince Littler, those two tremendously successful men who have reached such heights in theatrical business. Blanche, herself, knows more about theatrical affairs than most people in the business. For years she ran the Artillery Theatre, Woolwich, in conjunction with her brothers. She was considerably younger than George when they married but as her mother told me once, "Blanche always liked men much older than herself." I know very few people who are more charming than Lady Robey. Delightful to look at, amusing, witty, a woman of tremendous energy and drive. She took over the Red Cross in Brighton, after George died, and is never tired of organizing ways and means of collecting funds for that splendid charity. She possesses great business and financial ability, and I think it is no secret that she managed her husband's business affairs in a way that he never succeeded in doing so satisfactorily himself.

George knew success, knew popularity, realized that he reached the topmost rungs of the ladder which he set out to climb, but I doubt if any of the years of his phenomenal success were as happy as the later years of his life spent with

Blanche. She was his companion, his wife, and she mothered him without ever letting him realize that she did so. He still appeared from time to time in television, and spoke on the radio, he hated to be idle, and invented a game to keep his hands occupied. He became a past master at unravelling string! No matter how complicated the knots, George would work at them patiently until he untied them.

He had been given a C.B.E. at the end of the First World War for his services in the Volunteer Transport, for the work he had done for the wounded in hospital and for the unstinted help which he had given in raising money for many good causes. Then in February 1954 came the news that he was to receive a knighthood. He was nearly eighty-five and the honour was the recognition of a life of hard work, of spreading laughter, and never missing a single performance! That last was one of his few boasts.

He and Blanche went up to London. The Queen was on one of her tours through the Dominions, and the Queen Mother was taking her place. George and Blanche arrived at the Palace, where an equerry was waiting with a wheel-chair. George eyed it with disfavour.

"I've no intention of being wheeled up to the Queen Mother in that contraption," he said, "I'm perfectly able to walk."

The equerry very wisely made no protest—doubtless Blanche had caught his eye and if she had not actually "tipped him the wink" had at least conveyed a line of approach to him. He took it!

"I'm sorry you won't use it, Mr. Robey," he said, "it's the chair that Queen Mary always used when she was going to go round an exhibition or anything of that kind . . ."

George smoothed his chin, "Ah, Queen Mary, eh? A great lady. Well, if she used it, it would be churlish of me to refuse to do so."

He got in and very cleverly and swiftly he was almost whirled to within a yard or so of the Queen Mother. His name was announced, he walked forward and knelt, the sword was laid on his shoulder, and he mistimed his cue for probably the first time in his life. He began to rise to his feet, when the Queen Mother, cried urgently, "Mr. Robey, you're only half done!" George, covered with confusion knelt again and received the accolade in its complete form.

He was very proud of his knighthood, because he regarded it not only as a recognition of George Robey, but of the whole profession of which he was so proud.

Blanche's mother, Mrs. Littler, lived with them at their charming house at Rottingdean; the trio was a completely happy one, for Agnes Littler was a delightful woman, intelligent and possessing a great sense of humour.

One day, George said to her reflectively, "In my time I have sung a good many songs about mothers-in-law, made jokes concerning them. I would never do either if I had my time over again. But—" and he smiled, "when I sang them, I didn't know you!"

While Blanche's father was alive, he and George loved to indulge in what became a favourite pastime with them both. They would fire quotations at each other, and demand the name of the author. If one of them gave a quotation which was fairly well known, the other when giving the correct reply would jeer, that such an easy, infantile quotation should be given, protesting they were not worth the trouble of answering.

Blanche told me, "They both enjoyed catching the other out. My father was very good at the game, but George almost invariably beat him. It seemed to me that George had read everything! How he found the time to do so always remained a mystery to me."

I have his book—*Looking back on Life*—which is signed by both Blanche and him. There are pasted in two caricatures of George, drawn by himself, one as Sancho Panza, the other in that well-known semi-clerical garb, without a collar, and the little bowler hat.

That book has a strange history. I had it in my study, I was very proud of it, for my admiration of the Prime Minister

of Mirth had always been unbounded. Someone stole it. I
have never known who perpetrated such an abominable thing,
but my precious book had disappeared. In June, 1963, two
friends of mine were lunching with me, Bert Lytton, and Charles
Power. Both had belonged to the stage, Bert as a light comedian,
Charles had played in legitimate plays. The talk turned to the
Prime Minister of Mirth, and Charles asked me if I had read
his book?

"He and Blanche gave me a signed copy," I said, "and some
kind friend—took it!"

Charles nodded, "Would you like it back? If so I'll give it
to you."

"You will!" I stared. "But it disappeared from my villa in
Italy, you've never been there in your life, anyway you'd never
do a beastly thing like——"

He said, "Of course not. But you know my proclivity for
digging about second-hand book shops and buying anything
I can find dealing with the stage or the music halls. Well, I
found—your book."

He handed me the book neatly wrapped in brown paper.
There it was, a beautifully clean copy in its bright orange cover.
There were the caricatures, and there was the inscription.
"To Mickie" beside my name someone had written very neatly
in pencil, "Naomi Jacobs".

Charles said, "Someone who didn't know you very well, or
they'd have known how you hate to be called—Jacobs."

He told me that he had been "digging about", when the
orange cover caught his eye in a second-hand book shop. He
picked it up, read the inscription and decided that it should be
returned to its rightful owner. It is now back in its old home
here in Italy.

The last time I saw the "P.M." was in the late summer of
1954, I drove out to Rottingdean to see Blanche and him. He
was in bed, "Not very well—" but she insisted that he would
like to see me. He looked very frail I thought, but when Blanche
said, "Have you got a story for Mickie, George?" his eyes

twinkled. "I've always had a story for Mickie," he said, and told me one—a rather "naughty" story, speaking in the Welsh intonation, and told it with all his old verve and clarity. He might have laid aside the trappings of the Prime Minister of Mirth, but he still had the essential humour and artistry which earned him that name.

Among my collection of walking sticks, I have one of his little canes which he used on the stage. It is in good company, for there is one of Sir Gerald du Maurier's, one of Seymour Hicks', another which belonged to G. H. Chirgwin, the "White Eyed Kaffir", and carved by him, a head which he believed was a portrait of himself. There is one which Lionel Brough always used, given to me by his grand-daughter—and George Robey's cane.

I—in common with hundreds of thousands of others, admired him as a great comedy artiste, for his versatility, for his erudition, and his great humanity. He could never have portrayed many of the types he did, unless he had studied his fellow men and women with care, with amusement, with understanding and—sympathy.

X

HARDING CARTWRIGHT, MASTER MARINER

HE was never in the Birthday Honours or any other honours list that I know of, he was Commodore of his Line, and that a very fine fleet of ships known all over the Seven Seas and every port of any size in the world. He had achievements to his credit, and only under considerable persuasion and with a good deal of belittling of his own part in the stories would he talk about them. Then invariably it was the "other chap" who was held up as the hero.

If you want to hear the real stories about him, you must go to the smoking room of one of those hotels to be found in the big ports—Cape Town, Sidney, London, Liverpool, New York, or Glasgow—where Master Mariners congregate at the end of a long voyage and talk of the things they have seen, heard and experienced.

Don't imagine that you will find in these smoking rooms a crowd of those unkempt, untrimmed, sea-dogs who exist in the pages of romances of the sea. They are mostly, though here and there you may find an eccentric figure and character, quiet voiced, modest men, with very clear eyes, much wrinkled at the corners through screwing them up against sun, driving seas and fierce winds. They have firm mouths, jaw lines which speak of determination, and skins which are tanned by the elements. They affect neat, unobtrusive clothes when they are not actually wearing uniform, they do not invariably appear with a "pipe gripped firmly" in their teeth, neither is their inevitable drink rum and lemon.

These are the Master Mariners, the men who hold the tickets of extra-master, who are when aboard their ship absolute monarchs, whose word is law, in fact who actually become—the law! They have the safety of several hundred people in their hands, they must know how to mix with their passengers, to exercise diplomacy, to settle arguments, to make tactful suggestions which are in reality orders, to exercise discipline, and congratulate themselves only when a voyage is safely over, their ship safely docked, when passengers and crew have gone their various ways, that they have brought home what can be justly known as "a Happy Ship".

One of these men was my friend of many years' standing, Captain Harding Cartwright.

When I knew him first, he was a tall, well-built man, rather heavily built, immaculate in uniform and well dressed when he was ashore. He possessed what is known as "a square rigged ticket", which means that he qualified after serving an apprenticeship in one of the last of the old sailing vessels. I fancy that he told me that he served in a five-masted barque. It was a hard school, for the old captains believed in hardening their apprentices. Later they were known as junior officers, or cadets, then they were apprentices. Their parents or guardian paid considerable premiums for the privilege of their living in cramped quarters, of being soaked to the skin in bad weather with no chance of drying their garments except by waiting for the weather to clear, and then hanging them out to let the wind and sun do what they could.

Bugs were plentiful, and weevils were not unknown in the ship's biscuits. Voyages which took eighteen months or two years were common. Small wonder that boys "swallowed the anchor", and deserted the ship when they reached a port which was part of the British Empire.

That was how Harding Cartwright learned to be a seaman. Long voyages, microscopic pay, living rough, returning home to join some school for prospective Mercantile Marine officers and study for the necessary examinations. Those examinations were far from being child's play; true, according to their indentures the apprentices were promised instruction while at sea, that instruction to be given to them by a senior and already qualified officer. The promise was usually more honoured in the breach than the observance.

However young Harding passed all his examinations and gained his master's ticket. That did not satisfy him and he sat for what is known as an Extra Master's Ticket, something equivalent to an Honour's Degree.

He climbed the ordinary way, third mate, second and finally first officer, entitled to be addressed as "Mr. Cartwright" even by the Captain himself. Finally the day came when he was given his own ship and stood on the bridge with the pilot taking her out on his first voyage as captain. I can imagine his good-looking, fresh coloured face, topped by a head covered with curly hair which held more than a hint of red, his broad shoulders squared, trying to look completely at ease, and yet fully conscious that he was entering a new phase of his life. A phase which carried grave responsibilities, certain privileges, there would be quick decisions to make, judgements to give. He was empowered to perform a marriage ceremony should the occasion arise, it was his duty to officiate at the funeral of anyone who died at sea aboard his ship. He could pass judgement on anyone who transgressed the law of the ship, he could commit them to close confinement in irons if he deemed it necessary.

He may have given his cheerful grin when he thought of those irons and remembered the old sea law, that if the prisoner could find a single spot of rust on them, he had the right to demand their immediate removal. In every ship there was a sailor known as a "sea lawyer", usually elderly men who were only too delighted to quote obscure rules and regulations, some of them ages old, but which still held validity. Something of a trial to any captain, those sea lawyers.

He determined that any ship in which he sailed should be a "happy ship", more it should be kept "Ship-shape and Bristol fashion". He remembered the old rhyme learnt in his days of sail:

Six days shalt thou labour and do all that thou art able,
And on the seventh day holy-stone the deck and scrape the
  bloody cable.

Those had been rough old days, but they had taught him a
great deal, and he remembered them with a certain gratitude.

He wanted a "well found" ship, nothing makeshift about her.
He remembered how some of the smaller steam ships in which
he had served as mate, parsimonious owners were too mean to
provide the things necessary for running a vessel. Once in
particular he went down to the office in a port on the North
East Coast, to indent for some marlin-spikes. The owner, an
avaricious little man of German extraction, demanded, "Vat
d'you want?"

"To indent for some marlin-spikes, sir."

"Marlin-spikes! For vat? Don't you hev a poker in der
damned galley? Use that!"

So his career as a Master Mariner began, he sailed the whole
world over, and wherever his ship docked, Harding Cartwright made friends. Those early friendships—made in all
parts of the world—lasted for the whole of his life. When his
wife was dangerously ill in 1962, letters came every day from
friends neither she nor Harding had seen for over thirty years,
but who still kept in touch with them both.

He rose in position, and in the estimation of his owners,
and when the First World War broke out, he became
part and parcel of that "life line" which was so necessary to
Britain.

He sailed under sealed orders, Britain was at war, the seas
held an additional danger and a shot was fired across his bows.
"Stand to!" A German destroyer had waylaid him.

Harding shrugged his shoulders, and said to his Chief
Officer, "Temporarily—the game's up!" then as he saw the
boat-load of Germans approaching, he clapped his hand to his
forehead, "God! My orders".

He rushed to his cabin, took them from his safe, and tore

them into small pieces. Those he flung into the water-closet and pulled the chain. For the first time in Harding's memory it failed to work! He tried again, still no trickle of water! In the distance he could hear the loud hectoring voices of the German boarding party. He stooped down, gathered the pieces of paper into his hand, squeezed the water out of them, and—ate them.

When he told me the story I asked, "Not particularly pleasant?"

He grinned, "Damned tough!"

He was questioned by a very smart, very self-sufficient German officer.

"Are you the captain?"

"I'm the Master of this ship, yes."

"What's her name?"

"I don't remember, they re-christened her. The name has escaped me."

"Bound for——?"

"Sailing under sealed orders."

"Where are they? Hand them over."

Very blandly, with that particular brand of urbane blandness which North Countrymen can assume, Harding replied, "I couldn't tell you, I don't know."

"Thrown them over-board, eh?"

"Certainly not." He was almost indignant at the suggestion.

"*Donner!* Blockhead! Have you eaten them!"

A slow smile spread over Harding's face, as if the German had struck a chord in his memory, "Yes! That's exactly what I have done!"

His beloved ship with its officers and crew were taken prisoner, they were despatched to a prison camp. Their uniforms were taken from them and they were given some very old, remarkably dirty clothes in their place. A few days later they were paraded. The inspecting officer, immaculate and over-bearing, surveyed Harding Cartwright with distaste.

"So! And you are an officer! You look like a tramp!"

"Then give me back my uniform and give my officers theirs," Harding snapped.

The uniforms were returned, but by some oversight Harding was not asked to return the filthy garments he had been wearing previously. He hid them under his mattress, you never knew—

Parcels began to trickle through. By this time Harding had married, a woman with whom he was in love all his life. His "Jenny" remained his ideal woman always, she was allowed— in such high regard were both Harding and his wife held by the Owners—to take many voyages with him. I do not know if this is ever permitted in these days, but I remember at the time when Jane Cartwright went voyaging with her husband, that captains' wives were not usually regarded as unmixed blessings by the officers and crew. There were never any grumbles about Jane. She never interfered, never offered criticism unless it was helpful and constructive, she never attempted to "mother" the junior officers though she darned their socks and replaced lost buttons calmly, efficiently and without fuss.

At the beginning of a voyage Harding would be asked by one of his officers, "Mrs. Cartwright coming with us, sir?"

"Not this trip."

"Oh, bad luck, sir."

That was the usual comment when Jane remained in England, fighting some municipal or county council battle, generally with signal success. She was a notable cook, and out of the meagre rations allocated to the British people during the war, she saved and scraped, probably begged—I believe that she would have stolen for necessary ingredients to make a Christmas cake for Harding. He told me:

"I talked a lot about that cake. I knew what Jenny's cakes were like. Everyone else talked about it too. We were like kids waiting for Santa Claus. The others were expecting parcels, and we used to speculate as to what they might contain and how we would have a wonderful Christmas dinner. Even the German guard heard about that cake of mine. He wasn't a

bad chap, big, fair haired fellow from Saxony. The day came
—*Der Tag*, eh? He told me that it was a big parcel and grinned
all over his face. You had to open any parcel in front of an
N.C.O. in case your people had hidden money in a cake, or a
couple of battalions of the British Army, or a few machine
guns! There it was, a biscuit tin, all fastened most carefully.
The N.C.O.—what a pig he was too!—unfastened it, and took
out the contents, a big mince pie, chocolate slabs, cigarettes—
where on earth did my blessed Jenny get it all from?—and
finally the—Cake. I held my breath, and peered at it as it lay
safely at the bottom of the tin. A big, beautifully baked plum
cake, my mouth watered! The Hun stared at it, then gave a
nasty side-long look at me. He shrugged his shoulders, and
said, *Mein Gott—kinder! Dummkopf!* Then taking the tin he
raised it high above his head turned it upside down, and
shook it. The cake fell out on to the dirty counter, and smashed
into a thousand pieces!

"I saw red, I could have murdered him, and very cheerfully
too. I snatched the tin, and brought the open end down on his
head, pressing it down because it was a pretty tight fit, so that
he looked as if he was wearing a metal helmet. He cursed and
swore, in spite of my fury I began to laugh. He yelled for help,
other Huns came running, and most of them started laughing
too, they couldn't help it. One of them gave me a well-aimed
kick on the shin as he passed, but even he laughed. 'Never
miss the opportunity of kicking a prisoner' is a kind of axiom
with them. Or was then.

"Inside the tin the N.C.O. was getting hotter and hotter,
no one could budge the thing, and the hotter he got the tighter
it seemed to fit! Finally they had to get one of the camp
engineers to come and cut it off with special pliers.

"Of course I was hauled before the Camp Commander and
how I wished that I could have understood all the N.C.O.
said about the affair! However I have a pretty good imagination and tried to imagine what a British N.C.O. would have
said, and the very thought of it made me want to laugh.

However, the Camp Commander wasn't too bad a chap, and I saw even his eyes twinkle; he said something to the N.C.O. and the brute looked sulky so I imagine that it wasn't anything too pleasant, then he turned to me and in very bad English told me that I deserved to be punished, but that 'Christmas a time of goot veel iss' that made me want to giggle again, and so he would overlook my 'behaviour viceech so bad vas!'

"One of my companions in misfortune when I told the story said, 'You blasted fool, why didn't you gather up the crumbs? They would have been good enough to eat. They were British crumbs after all'."

The camp was very near a small town, and Harding discovered that as there was no dentist in the camp, or if any of the prisoners belonged to a dental unit they had no instruments with them, and that prisoners were allowed to visit the local dentist under escort.

Harding Cartwright told me that to be taken prisoner was the greatest disgrace that could befall a man who was taken while serving his country. It was something about which he felt very deeply and keenly. He began to plan an escape. He knew several men who had visited the dentist under escort, and although they said that the dentist was far from humane in his ministrations, yet he had managed to "yank" out an offending tooth after a few unsuccessful attempts. When he told me he said, his eyes dancing, "Do you remember that film Charles Laughton was in? *Henry VIII.* He said, 'The things I've done for England!' I felt like that!"

To the dentist then went Harding in company with two other men and a guard—an armed guard. Harding insisted that his comrades were attended to first and stayed talking to the girl who had opened the door to them. The guards muttering that they were only going to stand outside the door and smoke, disappeared.

Harding repeated that he talked to the girl, adding, "She was a very pretty girl, very pretty!" in a tone which spoke, and was doubtless intended to speak, volumes.

Jane who had doubtless heard the story before said, "Harding!" in a voice which was "meaningful" and slightly over-played.

The other two Englishmen returned from the dentist's clutches, and Harding went in and demanded a filling. Then he protested that he could stand no more after the drilling and must return the following week. The next time, one of his companions said as they marched to the dentist's, "You're putting on weight, Cartwright." Harding agreed and said that it was due to the badly regulated diet. The filthy old coat and trousers had come in useful, even though they did spoil the set of his uniform trousers. He was always something of a "dandy" about his clothes. Again Harding insisted that his friends went in to the dentist first, again the guards went out "to smoke", again the pretty girl remained talking to the nice Englishman.

With becoming modesty, and in very halting German, he asked her leave to absent himself for a moment or two. With a certain amount of pantomime he conveyed that the camp food was very bad, and that he had a delicate stomach and—and—and——

The girl sympathized, and showed him the room which he needed. The door locked, off came the decent uniform, the trousers, and instead of a Master Mariner there stood a scruffy looking fellow wearing disgracefully old and dirty clothes.

"The window was a tight fit," he told me, "but I managed to wriggle through. No, it wasn't a pleasant journey, but—I got home eventually."

Between the First and Second World Wars Harding retired, his heart was not in good condition, the German prison camp had not improved it, and he had, I think, two bad attacks of pneumonia. The second war broke out, and although his doctor and his wife both advised against it, he rejoined his old company. He took out several convoys to South Africa, and if any reader travelled in a convoy and possessed the smallest imagination, they can readily imagine the strain which is felt by the Commodore, the weight of dreadful responsibility which is laid on his shoulders.

Had his physical heart been half as sound as his mental and spiritual heart was, he would have gone on for the duration. The spirit was as willing as it had always been, it was the "flesh" which betrayed him. He'd beaten the sea in its worst and most dangerous moods, he'd fought the elements and come through all his encounters with a "clean ticket", he had even beaten the Germans when they tried to hold him, but his years defeated him. He had to hand in his resignation. That must have been the hardest blow he ever had to face, and he faced it with courage and determination. He went back to the house which Jane and he had built, where were gathered all the things which they had collected on their travels together—carpets from the East, that magnificent Kandy chest with its ornate brass corners and elaborate lock, books, and the rest. There were the model ships which Harding had made during long voyages to amuse himself and there, not five hundred yards away beyond the sand dunes, was the sea.

The order came that all houses along the sea front must be evacuated, they would be requistioned by the Army and the Air Force. He and Jane moved inland, they tried living in a boarding house, and hated it! Then they found a cottage, a charming place which they took, and where they lived for some time until they might return to their own home.

Harding began to fret, tugging at his moorings. He hated the sense of—doing nothing. He joined the Home Guard, was put in command of it in that district and prepared to work heart and soul at the work of organizing it. I remember going up to stay with them for a week-end and marvelling at his energy and enthusiasm. He had been told to prepare for evacuees, a considerable number of them.

There was a village hall, some chairs and tables and nothing else provided. He spent hours making lists of requirements, rushed about getting people to promise to lend what was needed. No information was forthcoming as to the numbers he might expect, their sex, or how long they might be staying; so Harding went blindly on collecting promises and wearing out that heart which was already ready to give trouble if too much strain was put upon it.

Jane helped, of course Jane helped, she never failed to do that, but it was a heartbreaking assignment for a man of Harding's temperament.

I was due to go overseas at the time, and I remember the day I left the delightful cottage and my two dear friends. A car was coming to drive me to the nearest big town. I was upstairs doing my packing. It was just finished when there was a knock on the door. Jane and Harding walked in. He said in that deep, warm voice of his, "Well, you're going overseas, and its hard to say when we shall be together again. We're all facing a bad time, whether we're in one of the Services or not. Jane and I just felt we'd like to ask God, if it's His will, to let us all meet again—in happier times."

We knelt down by the side of the bed, both Jane and Harding said a prayer, very short, very simple and very sincere. I have rarely been so moved. There were two people, my dear friends, both people who loved gaiety, fun, laughter, kneeling "in the faith of Little Children" asking for protection for us all.

None of us ever mentioned the incident again. Neither of them have ever "talked religion" to me, for I do not belong to their church, but I know that they have both always had unshakable faith, and have held fast to the simple Faith which is surely the essence of true religion.

The war ended, and Jane and Harding went back to their own home to find that it had suffered considerably, not at the hands of the Germans, but regrettably at the hands of the troops which had been billeted there. Harding, eyeing the amount allowed to him by a grateful Government for repairs and re-placements, said wryly, "They must expect me to buy everything from Woolworth's—which in those days sold everything at 6d. and 3d. —from basins, to new skirting boards!"

Jane said cheerfully, "Don't worry, Harding, we'll manage."

And manage they did. The house became itself again, the garden bloomed, their old friends came flocking back to see them and talk over war experiences. Both of them had felt the effects of the long war, both of them had fretted at having to live in houses which were not their own, they had both suffered serious illnesses.

They admitted—with great cheerfulness—that "we're old people, and we've got to face it, and adjust our lives". Jane broke her hip and had to walk with the aid of a stick, Harding invested in a "deaf aid", and when I asked him last summer if it was any good, he chuckled.

"Well there's several kinds of—good," he said, "there's good, and there's—no good. It's somewhere between the two." Still they remained unfailingly cheerful, regarding the fact that Jane was over eighty and Harding only a very few years younger as if it were something of a personal achievement.

The last time I visited them Harding and I commiserated with one another that our respective doctors no longer allow us to enjoy a whisky and soda!

Jane said, "And a very good thing too!" unfeelingly.

Harding added, "Look at the money we save!"

They both came to the gate to see me drive off, both waving and Harding calling, "Next year! And stop a little longer, both of you."

I watched them as we drove away, and Sara said, "What a gallant couple they make."

Ten days ago came a letter from Jane, written in her characteristic firm, bold handwriting. Harding was very ill. In hospital. Then in a week another letter. The Master Mariner had set out on his last voyage. "Before he became unconscious," Jane wrote, "he said to me, 'I hope to see my pilot face to face, when I have crossed the bar'."

I thought, "Not a bad exit line for a Master Mariner" and felt certain that he'd get safely to a good harbour.

XI

LESLIE FABER and GODFREY TEARLE

THEY were both actors, and content to be actors. They had no particular yearnings to write their lives for the delectation of the general public, they did not aspire to be champion golfers, or painters, they were proud of their profession and of the fact that they belonged to it.

Godfrey Tearle came from a theatrical family, his father Osmund Tearle and his uncle Edmund were both actors of considerable note particularly in the provinces; Godfrey's father also made a success both in South Africa and in America. It was in New York in 1884 that Godfrey Tearle was born.

Coming as he did from a family steeped in theatrical tradition, there were no objections raised when Godfrey announced his intention of becoming an actor and joining his father's touring company. He made his first appearance in Burnley. He continued to tour with his father until the latter's death in 1901.

Godfrey then toured the provinces in repertory, and having already been trained under the tutelage of his father, a very sound if uninspired actor, he never picked up those "repertory tricks" which have continued to mar the performances of so many actors and actresses long after they have left repertory behind them.

He made his first London appearance at the King's, Hammersmith, when he played the Earl of Bothwell to Mrs. Brown Potter's Queen of Scots.

From then he was rarely out of the West End theatres, he was well built, handsome, and his voice, one of the finest I have ever heard, rivalled that of Henry Ainley, whose voice was acclaimed as one of the most beautiful voices ever heard on the English Stage. Godfrey Tearle ran him very close!

I think that the first time I ever saw him was in *The Garden of Allah*, when I remember he had an astonishingly long speech to make. I felt at the time, this was in 1921, that in the hands of a lesser artist that speech might have killed the play, and inexperienced though I was, I realized with admiration how Tearle "broke up" that long, and admittedly tedious speech so that the interest of the audience was kept alive.

I saw him in *The Way of an Eagle*, a rather preposterous play, in which the producer may have been admirable in many ways, but his knowledge of fox-hunting and its usages were non-existent. What struck me in that play was that Godfrey Tearle, playing not only with artistry but with complete sincerity, made you forget all the solecisms and accept things which, had the part been played by a lesser artist, would have moved you to laughter.

I saw him in many plays, in a variety of parts, all of which he acted with distinction. His stage presence was little short of magnificent, and that beautiful voice, which was always under perfect control made his performances memorable.

I remember very well that "obstinately successful" play, *White Cargo*, which ran so long that three different actors in turn played the leading part. The first was Franklin Dyall, a fine actor, capable of making the most incredibly sinister characters completely credible. He played Meister in *The Ringer*, a traditionally correct stage villain. In the hands of a less good actor, he would have degenerated into a real "stock" character. I heard, for I was in *The Ringer* myself, some of the younger actors and even members of the audience say, "Dyall's work gets awfully ham!"

My reply was always the same, "Possibly according to your standards you may be right, but what wonderfully good and effective 'ham' it is!"

Then Franklin left the play to open in some new production for which he was already contracted, he was followed in *White*

Cargo by Godfrey Tearle. No two actors could have interpreted the part so differently, and probably more skilfully. Dyall had been cynical, disillusioned, life held nothing for him except the endless round of watching young men come out to the lonely, uncomfortable station full of determination to reorganize the living conditions, to make the quarters cleaner, even more attractive, and most of all to do nothing which could sully the reputation or lower the moral rectitude of the Britons who have come to shoulder "the white man's burden".

Dyall had grown cynical and cultivated his cynicism as a kind of armour against disappointment. Tearle hated the cynicism which circumstances had almost forced upon him. Dyall listened to the enthusiastic plans of the newcomers with a sneer which he did not attempt to hide. He had watched so many "high hopes faint on a cold hearth-stone", seen so many cases where conventional morality had weakened and finally crashed to pieces. He would have suffered a form of disappointment if the newest importation had not come out voicing high hopes, and firm intentions destined never to be fulfilled.

Tearle on the other hand, had grown cynical and almost hated himself for having become so. He knew that the plans for improvement, the determination to avoid any association with native women could weaken and if he sneered, you felt it was to protect himself against his own secret disappointment. Dyall portrayed a man who had grown sour, Tearle gave us one who had become bitter because he too had longed to make his ideals actualities many years ago.

Godfrey was leaving *White Cargo* to go to a new production as Franklin Dyall had done, and Leslie Faber was to take the part which they had both played so admirably.

I went with him to watch Godfrey play the part for almost the last time. Leslie Faber watched and listened intently. When the last curtain fell, he said to me, "So long as we have acting like Godfrey's on the English stage—there will be nothing very wrong with it! God, what an actor he is!"

When he played the part, it differed again from either Dyall's or Tearle's interpretation. He played it as a man who listened to the hopes and plans of the newest arrival with an air of bored, almost sleepy indifference. He had heard it all so often, he had watched the same denouement so often, he was tired of it, and bored by it. Only at rare intervals did he rouse himself to voice some coldly, cynical comment which stung the newcomer like a whip-lash. When he spoke his last line, it did not carry a tone of regret, of indignation that the climate, the loneliness, the general discomforts were too much for young, untried men, there was no hint of "The pity of it all!" Rather it was a cold comment on the inevitability of everything, the acceptance that the dice had been loaded against the young man by Fate from the moment he set foot on the station.

It is an interesting memory to have seen those three men play the same part and to notice how differently they treated it. I have heard people say, with that air of profundity with which the "laity" speak of stage matters, "There can only be one way to play a part or possibly two. The right way and the wrong way." That, of course is childish nonsense and like so much childish nonsense gets far more attention than it deserves.

White Cargo was the last part which Leslie Faber was destined to play, not the stage version, but the film which was made of it. Indeed he never quite finished the film, there were still a few lines of the sound track to be spoken. (It may be that they produce "talkies" differently in 1964, but in those days the sound track was independently produced, or it was in this particular film.)

I remember going to the private showing of the film. It was shown at a cinema in Regent Street. The cinema was packed, the majority of the audience were stage people, most of us had been some weeks before to the memorial service for Leslie Faber at St. Martin's in the Fields, and waiting to see him on the screen, to hear his voice, was a strange and very disturbing experience. I remember Gerald du Maurier, that actor, who

LESLIE FABER AND GODFREY TEARLE

in those parts which he had made particularly his own was inimitable. You rarely saw him in any other type of part, for the simple reason that the public adored him in "Gerald du Maurier parts" and were disappointed if he attempted to give them any other.

I remember seeing him that morning before the film began, sitting very tense and obviously feeling that the occasion was going to prove difficult for a man who had been one of Leslie's closest friends. I believe that the actor—whose name I entirely forget, if indeed I ever knew it, who was called in to finish the sound track, stated that the voice was his all through the film; Nigel Bruce assured me that it amounted to some two dozen words. They came at the end of the film. Gerald had watched it and it certainly was not a good film, in silence, until the last couple of lines came which were not spoken by Leslie, and were the "tag" of the play. Then he said, loudly and clearly, "That's not Faber's voice. The inflexion is wrong. Faber never used a wrong inflexion!"

To return to Godfrey Tearle, I had known him for a long time, but I came to know him really well, when he came out with the E.N.S.A. Festival Players to Italy towards the end of the war. E.N.S.A. sent out *The Apple Cart*, *The Amazing Doctor Clitterhouse*, and, I think, *Who Killed the Count*. Godfrey played Clitterhouse which was an enormous success with the troops. *The Apple Cart* as they said themselves, "left them cold".

On the first night at Trieste they opened with this play and I went with Godfrey to see it. It was part of my work to get the reaction of the audience to the various shows which were sent out. The play was beautifully acted and the audience were profoundly bored. Towards the end of the last act the theatre was half empty. I went to the main entrance to talk to some of the men as they came out. Godfrey came with me, curious to know what they would have to say. Two soldiers came out and I asked them how they had enjoyed the show? One of them, a Cockney, was enthusiastic.

"Orlrite! Mind you, I'm in-ter-*ested* in politiks. Unnerstand the delusions, w'eer some mite not, if you git me. I spotted that chap in the 'igh boots minnit 'e came on. Said to my pal, 'Joe Stalin!', didn't I, mate?"

"You did," the other said gloomily.

"Reckernised a lot of 'oo they was meant ter be. 'Ow long ago did Shaw write this play, ma'am?"

I said, "I'm not sure of the exact date, about 1930, I think." He stared at me, then said, "Coo! An' I thought it was tropical! Jest goes ter show you."

Godfrey was very tired on that tour and when I found that I had a free week-end after the Trieste week, and that the company did not open in Milano until the following Tuesday, I asked him if he would care to spend the weekend at my villa in Sirmione. In his usual thoughtful fashion his first question was, "Are you sure that I shan't be a bother to you?" Assured that I should not allow him to be that, he accepted, and as he was not playing on the Saturday, we left Trieste early on the Saturday arriving at Sirmione in time for tea. During those three days he rested and I realized that although he looked fit and well, he was almost exhausted. When I drove back to Milano with him on the Tuesday he looked revitalized. I went on to Rome with the company, and had the joy of showing Godfrey something of the Immortal City.

There were several young actresses in the company and I shall never forget how kind he was to them. There was no patronizing by a "star artiste" towards "small fry", there was no favouritism, he might have been a very handsome, kindly uncle taking his nieces about, intent upon giving them a really good time.

One evening after the performance, he and I went out to supper at Alfredo's. I think that he was leaving for England the next day, or I was leaving Rome; anyhow, we sat and talked until the not-too-early-hours, and he told me how much he had enjoyed his tour, adding, "I don't suppose I shall have another chance of seeing Italy."

"My villa's always there, come when you like——" I said. He smiled, "I believe that you really mean that. I shall do my best."

Later he wrote to me from England, thanking me for what I had done for the comfort of the artists, and adding, "You have tried to give us a real picture of the country, shown us wonderful things we might never have found for ourselves. Thank you most of all for being—Mickie."

He died rather suddenly, though he had actually been a sick man for quite a long time, and the stage lost an actor who was one of its greatest ornaments. I have never heard anyone, in the theatrical profession or out of it, who spoke of Godfrey Tearle in any way but with affection and admiration. As an actor he was great, as a man he was "without guile". He had that simplicity which only people of outstandingly fine characters possess. He found genuine "fun" in small things, there was no necessity to offer him elaborate schemes for his entertainment. "Books, and my food and summer-rain", good company, warm friendliness made him perfectly happy. His range as an actor was wide, his sense of humour no one who saw him in *The Light of Heart*—despite its tragic ending—could doubt, was admirable.

I never felt that he was at his best in plays which were of the "drawing-room comedy" type, he needed more vivid colours, parts which bordered on the eccentric or unconventional. He played Shakespeare splendidly, his fine voice and beautiful diction giving the words their full value, playing with restraint and yet never afraid of allowing himself an outburst when the play demanded it. Godfrey Tearle was indeed, a "well graced actor".

I have chosen to write of both Godfrey Tearle and Leslie Faber in the same chapter of this book, for two reasons, perhaps three. Both were good friends of mine, both were masters of their profession, that profession which I loved and still love, and concerning which I have some actual knowledge. You don't serve an apprenticeship with Robert Courtneidge as I did for nothing! Also because they both possessed the ability to play an enormous range of characters and to play them all excellently. Neither of them ever suffered from one of the greatest curses of the present-day stage—type casting. No casting director ever had to wonder *if* either of them could play this part or that. It was not a question of what either of them *could* play, the difficulty would have been to find a part which either of them could *not* play, and play with distinction.

The last time I talked with Ronald Squire was in his dressing room during a matinée. He did not appear in one of the acts, the play itself bored me. Ronnie Squire never had the ability to do that, so I spent the act in which he did not appear, in his dressing room.

I asked him, "Who in your opinion is the finest actor of your generation? Not the one you liked the best, but the one who in your considered opinion has the greatest claim to being called— great?"

Without a moment's hesitation, Ronnie answered, "Leslie Faber."

"Why?"

"Look at his range! Think of the parts he played—Lomond in *The Ringer*, the doctor in *The Outsider*, Tom Power in *Outward Bound*. Look at his performance in *The Letter* with Gladys Cooper, do you remember that exquisite performance of his in *By Candle-light*? What a gem that was!"

"You and Yvonne Arnaud were pretty large contributors to that success," I reminded him.

"Ah, Yvonne! She adorned everything she played. She'd have been superb in *East Lynne*." We both chuckled at the idea. "What she would have done with 'Lady Isobel', and——" a long pause, "she'd have made you believe in the woman! But it was Leslie who made us the combination that we were! You see both Yvonne and he adored their work, they knew that we had a gem of a play, and that the more it was polished the more it would sparkle! Now, I'm a lazy so-and-so, I do my work, enjoy doing it, then I want to get away to the Club. They'd have stayed there all night and every night, after every performance arguing over some line, some exit, some inflexion, debating why there wasn't a laugh on this line or that. Hours of it! But, they made the play that thing of perfection, or as near to perfection as anything we're any of us ever likely to see again."

We remembered other plays, *Jane Clegg* with dear Sybil Thorndike, when Leslie came to me one day telling me that he was worried about Clegg's continual cigarette smoking.

"What is he to do with the ash? Jane Clegg would never have allowed him to knock it on to the floor, I don't believe that people like the Cleggs have ash trays all over the place—what the devil am I to do with the ash?"

I thought for a moment, then said, "Knock it into the turn-up of your trousers."

He did, and the audience laughed, after that you might have imagined that I had been personally responsible for making Leslie's part a success. Any suggestion which you could make, if he felt that it added to the value of the characterization of the part, was received by him as a piece of genius.

Ronald Squire was right, his ability to play parts which were completely different was astonishing, and to each one he brought something which added to the richness of the character. I remember when *Excelsior* was put on at the Playhouse under Gladys Cooper's management, Ernest Thesiger played the part of Stanislas, an aristocrat who, for a fee, taught aspiring young women the way to make themselves a social success. Ernest, a very polished and altogether admirable actor played the part beautifully, he was the epitome of the polished aristocrat, cold, calculating, utterly without heart, working for one thing only, the social—and financial—success of his pupil. Leslie Faber had played Stanislas at a Sunday performance, but was unable to play it for the run of the play at The Playhouse because of a previous contract. I saw him on the Sunday night production.

He was as correct as Ernest Thesiger, as aristocratic, as capable of directing Gladys Cooper on her journey to social success, the possession of beautiful clothes, ropes of pearls and an exotic apartment in the most exclusive part of Paris; but under all his cold calculations there was the hint of a certain warmth, a faint trace of regret that this beautiful girl should leave her devoted, romantic and impecunious young lover in order to take for her motto the cry, "Excelsior". There was in his performance a strain of tolerant, half amused humour, a sort of mental "What fools these mortals be!" The Stanislas of Thesiger you might admire as a successful exponent of a slightly ignoble profession, Leslie Faber, while forcing you to admire his technique in the development of "Ginette", roused in you a kind of sneaking affection.

When he played Dr. Lomond in Edgar Wallace's *The Ringer*, he had to play the part with a Scottish accent. His beautiful wife, Gladys Grey, would ask me to dinner, and add, "Please give Leslie a lesson in speaking with a Scottish accent." When the play was produced Leslie sent me a photograph of himself as Dr. Lomond inscribed, "Very gratefully, Leslie."

When the play opened he was disguised as a very elderly man, grey hair, a pronounced stoop and a slow, exact type of speech. In the last act he had to snatch off his wig and appear as he was, an exceedingly handsome man of early middle age.

After each act he would remove some of the marks of age which he had painted on his face when he made up for the previous act. So skilfully did he do this, that when he stood before the audience wearing only an ordinary "straight" make-up because the change had been made so gradually and so carefully, they never realized that actually with each act Leslie had looked a little younger. The slow, rather precise enunciation had gone, and his voice rang out, the voice of a man in the very prime of life. The Scottish accent had gone and he stood there, upright, handsome, speaking in the voice audiences recognized as that of Leslie Faber.

In *The Letter*, he had to cross-question Gladys Cooper, who was suspected and very strongly suspected of murder. She sat at a plain wooden table on an ordinary kitchen chair, Leslie stood with his back to the audience. He always held that an actor should be able to "act with his back" and he achieved it in that scene. His voice came crisp, clear cut, and moderate in tone, as he questioned her. It was cold, very calm and rather aloof, utterly devoid of any emotion.

Suddenly she turned on him and asked furiously and with a touch of hysteria, "Why are you asking me all these questions?"

For the first time Leslie's voice was raised very slightly, but the tone cut like the lash of a whip.

"Can't you see that I'm only trying to save your neck?" There was the faintest pause before he spoke the work "neck", and it sent a shudder down your spine, you felt that you understood why Gladys stared at him for a second, terrified, wide-eyed, then rolled off the chair to the floor in a dead faint. Incidentally it was one of the most wonderfully executed falls I have ever seen on any stage.

I was in the cast when Leslie played in *The Spider* at the Winter Gardens. It was one of those uncomfortable plays, both for the actors and the audience, where half the actual "plot" is played from the auditorium by actors who are apparently part of the audience. I was one of them, a Woman in the stalls, who insists, after the crime has been committed in the audience when a man is shot (Basil Loder played the part) and the police forbid anyone to leave the theatre, that she must go home to her baby.

I remember that one of my lines was, "If there are any mothers in the audience, they will realize why it is absolutely necessary for me to be home by half-past nine precisely." The Duke and Duchess of York (King George VI and the present Queen Mother) were in the stalls, and I can still recall how she laughed at that line! Leslie played a conjurer, the "top of the bill" in a music hall. He came on wearing a cloak lined with red silk, flung it to a waiting assistant and proceeded to do some tricks. He did them remarkably well too, with some very witty patter. It wasn't really a part worthy of him, but he played it very smoothly and effectively. In the cast was

Lennox Pawle, an actor who was very successful in London, and equally so in America. He was a delightful man and a good friend of mine, but he was very often late for his cues. He played the manager of the "supposed" theatre, and looked exactly like Frank Boor who used to be manager of the London Hippodrome.

One evening I had to race down to the orchestra rails, and beseech Lennox (as the manager) to let me go home. One night he was late and Leslie was on the stage alone. I rushed down, shouting, "I demand to speak to the manager!" thinking that might reach Lennox's ears and bring him on to the stage. No Lennox! I clutched the orchestra rail and addressed myself to Leslie.

"You, sir, are the top of the bill, the star turn," peering into the wings hoping to see Lennox. "You are a person of importance, and so *in the absence of the manager* I appeal to you (another agonized look towards the wings for Lennox). I am sure, sir, that you cannot be so lost to all sense of——"

Leslie stood listening, looking the picture of misery. I had known the music halls, I had learnt to "gag", he had never "gagged" in his life, and would have hated to do so. I seemed to have been talking for literally hours, when Lennox rushed on, and told me to go back to my stall and behave myself.

I was scarcely back in my dressing-room after the fall of the curtain before both Leslie Faber and Lennox Pawle were knocking at the door, offering abject apologies, Lennox for not being there for his cue, Leslie because as he protested, "I've never been able to 'gag' in my life. You were wonderful! Superb!"

The next day my dressing room looked like a First Night, they had both sent me masses of flowers; Leslie's card was inscribed, "a token of my gratitude and admiration." Lennox's "An excellent speech. Shall never hesitate to miss my cue again."

Leslie always longed to play Lear, and had studied the part for several years. He always said that to play Lear properly,

LESLIE FABER AND GODFREY TEARLE

you must be too old in years and experience to play at all. I saw him play Richard II for a Sunday performance. I have seen many actors play the part, some good, some quite dreadful. Only two stand out in my memory as being worthy of remembrance, Leslie Faber's and John Gielgud's. When I told John Gielgud that, after I had seen his Richard, he said gravely, "You know as well as I do, whom I have to thank if my performance is worth watching."

There was no need for John to tell me, I knew—Leslie Faber. Both of them played that beautiful little scene with the Queen quite exquisitely, both of them played the Westminster Hall scene with wonderful dignity, and pathos which never drifted into being pity for themselves. One of Leslie's favourite admonishments was, "Never expect the audience to pity you, if they feel that you pity yourself." Neither of them made the king a stupid "fop", a harsh ingrate, an addle-pated babbler, a spoilt and capricious half-wit, they made him, as I for one, am convinced Shakespeare intended him to be, a man of ideals, one possessing many attributes which we have come to regard as "kingly", but totally unfitted to be a ruler of a veritable army of unscrupulous and immensely powerful lords.

Leslie Faber threw himself whole-heartedly into every character he played. Gladys Faber once said to me, "I'm always rather relieved when Leslie signs a contract to play a quiet part. They absorb him so completely, his parts, that he plays them 'on' and 'off'. For instance when he plays a stern, rugged type of man, he marches heavily about the house, speaks abruptly, doors bang, and he is always emphatic! When he played *By Candle-light*, he almost exuded charm, he smiled easily, and treated everyone with most wonderful courtesy."

Once, when Mrs. Patrick Campbell was dining with Gladys and Leslie in that charming house they had in Gloucester Place, she said to him "Why have you never chosen me to play in anything you were producing?" Leslie, who admired her profoundly and admitted that as a woman she frightened him to death, said, "Well, Mrs. Campbell, you know that you have a reputation for being very difficult——"

She cut him short indignantly, "Difficult! What nonsense! I should not call myself an *easy* woman for that implies immorality, but I am certainly not—what did you say?—difficult!"

I have written my opinion of Godfrey Tearle and Leslie Faber both as men and as actors, I have included them in the same chapter because they belonged to the same era. I suppose that in these days they might be regarded as rather old-fashioned, holding the belief, as they did, that the audience have a right to hear the words which the author had written. They both took their work seriously, both believed that they belonged to a very splendid profession, and they wished to be worthy of its traditions. The dignity of their calling was important to them both, neither had the slightest talent for self-advertisement or publicity.

I remember the day Leslie Faber was married to Gladys Grey. The ceremony was very quiet, only half a dozen people were present. The moment the ceremony was over, Leslie took Gladys' arm and said in a hoarse whisper, "There's a short cut I've discovered to Victoria. No one will see us! Good-bye, everyone, come, Gladys!"—and they hurried away diving down some narrow passage which Leslie had discovered, on their way to catch their train for the South of France.

Both Faber and Tearle died while still comparatively young, both were at the very height of their powers as actors, both left a record of brilliantly played parts, and to those people who knew them both well and intimately, they left the memory of themselves as men it was good to have known.

SIRMIONE,
ITALY.
1964.